HAU . . . . . .
WIRRAL

VOLUME TWO

Published by The Bluecoat Press, Liverpool
Book design by March Graphic Design Studio, Liverpool
Cover illustration by Tim Webster
Printed by Grafo

ISBN 9781904438816

THE BLUECOAT PRESS
3 Brick Street
Liverpool L1 0BL

Telephone 0151 707 2390
Website www.bluecoatpress.co.uk

Front cover *Strange Apparitions*, page 134

TOM SLEMEN

HAUNTED WIRRAL

VOLUME TWO

THE BLUECOAT PRESS

CONTENTS

Prenton Haunting

In the late spring of 2006, a family living at a rather average three-bedroomed house on Prenton Dell Road, set off for a fortnight's holiday in Spain, leaving Marcia, a forty-nine-year-old family friend, looking after their home whilst they were away. Marcia lived over the water in Liverpool with her husband Dave, but their marriage was on the rocks, and so they were quite grateful for the opportunity to live apart for a couple of weeks. Marcia stayed over in Prenton, and rarely telephoned home. She didn't wish to speak to her husband and since they had no children or pets, there was no reason to telephone her Aigburth home.

The first day at the semi-detached property was fairly uneventful. Marcia popped out to the newsagents and purchased a magazine and a bar of chocolate. After finishing both, she sat watching television for a while, until around 10pm, after which she went into the front parlour, which was across the hall, to read a book, settling herself into a comfortable winged armchair. In fact, she was so comfortable that, by about 11pm, the book had fallen from her lap and she had dozed off.

She was awakened with a start at 1.30am, by the sound of footsteps outside. They were coming towards the house, and as the rhythmic steps intensified, the silhouette of the late-night walker was projected on to the drawn curtains, its shape grotesquely distorted by the folds. The figure walked right up to the ground floor window, until its silhouette filled the entire right-hand pane, but it didn't stop there. The shadow passed straight through the window – its lower legs and feet going through the solid wall – and then walked across the room until it was within a few feet of Marcia, who was quaking with fear. She watched, dumbstruck, as the shadowy ghost then proceeded to walk into the next room, where it could be heard pacing around, as if looking for someone or something.

What was it doing? and why had it chosen this house? Marcia was far too terrified to go and investigate and, suddenly desperate to get out of the house, she leapt out of the armchair and ran out of the room and across the hall, where she tried to open the front door, forgetting she had bolted it earlier. She fumbled clumsily with the bolt and after what seemed like an age, managed to open the door and run outside. She looked about her to see if there was anyone who could help, but the street was silent and deserted. The cold night air soon had a sobering effect on her shattered nerves and although she felt an urge to wake up one of the neighbours to tell them about the incredible incident that had just taken place, she quickly realised that she would be branded a crank.

So she stood at the end of the garden path by the front gate, shivering in a tee shirt and shorts, considering what to do next. Eventually, she decided that she had no alternative but to go back inside, although every nerve in her body was telling her otherwise. She gingerly pushed open the front door and tiptoed back into the house, switching on every light as she did so. She stood in the hallway for quite some time with the front door ajar – just in case she had to make another swift getaway, in the event of a second encounter with the ghost. The radio in the kitchen was switched on for reassurance, quickly followed by the television and there was no sign of the apparition.

As the night wore on, Marcia began to persuade herself that she had simply experienced a particularly lucid dream, but the memory of the ghost was too fresh and too real and she dismissed the possibility.

By 7am Marcia was so exhausted that she had to go to bed, but she was still much too anxious to fall into a deep sleep. Two hours later she was rudely awakened from this dozing by the telephone ringing. It was Gemma, the mother of the family holidaying in the Costa del Sol. She had called to find out if everything was okay. Marcia hesitated for a moment, wondering whether to tell her of the ghostly visitation. In the end she decided not to, and simply said, "Yes, don't worry, everything's fine, love," and then asked the customary questions about the weather in Spain, the food, and so on.

As soon as Marcia had hung up, she lay face down in the bed and was trying to get back to sleep when she heard the distinctive bleep from her mobile phone. It was a text message. She wondered if it was from her husband, then decided it might be from Lindsey, her close friend in Liverpool, and so she lazily reached for the mobile on the bedside table. She took a look at the screen and pressed a key to read the message, which simply read: 'Kezzy Williams died this morning'.

For some reason, Marcia went cold when she read the text message. She didn't know anyone named Kezzy Williams, but somehow knew that it wasn't simply a message sent to her by accident by someone unknown to her. She searched the screen for the number of the sender of the bleak text, but there was none, which, again, didn't add up.

Suddenly, a floorboard in the bedroom creaked – just once – and Marcia tightened. She felt a powerful presence – a deeply masculine presence. She squeezed her eyes shut and felt her heart pound. Someone was definitely in the room, but she was too afraid to turn over and look. She muttered a rapid prayer and gulped. A vaguely familiar aroma permeated her nostrils. It was a sharp sweet smell; a comforting smell that instantly took Marcia back to her childhood, for it was the scent of her father's cologne which he always splashed on after shaving. It gave her the courage to turn over, and she sat up in bed to find that the room was empty. She wondered if her imagination was getting the better of her and drifted back off to sleep, rather uneasily, propped up against two pillows.

By noon, Marcia was up and sipping coffee in the kitchen. Although it was sunny outside, she felt a strange gloom hanging over the whole house, and she was unable to drive the memory of the shadow man walking through the window out of her mind. At 5pm Marcia received another call on her mobile that turned her blood to ice. This time it was her friend Lindsey and she was the bearer of some terrible news: Kerry Owens, a mutual schoolfriend, had died down in London, in the early hours of that morning, from a suspected heart attack. She had only been forty-seven. Marcia suddenly recalled the mysterious text message she had received earlier that morning, and told Lindsey about it. There was a pause, then Lindsey remarked, "Well that's Kerry's married name. You know ... she married Terry Williams and his pet name for her was Kezzy."

"Oh, my God!" said Marcia putting her hand to her mouth. Who could have texted that message earlier on?

As if that wasn't enough, there were more shocks in store for poor Marcia that day. Just before 9pm, she was sitting in the lounge, flicking through a myriad of tedious cable channels, when she thought she heard a voice coming from the front parlour. She muted the television, then slowly crept into the hall to the door opposite. She held her ear to the door. Yes, there was definitely a voice coming from somewhere. She stood stock still, listening. There was the voice again – without a doubt coming from the front parlour. Marcia felt light-headed as a hot rush of adrenaline shot through her veins. Finding courage from somewhere, she grasped the door handle and noiselessly twisted it. She opened it a crack, and immediately recoiled at the sound of a gravelly voice muttering within. In the centre of the twilit room stood an old woman with a shock of white hair. Her eyes were blue and cloudy and she was dressed in a cardigan and knee-length skirt of slate grey.

"Who the hell are you?" demanded Marcia, throwing open the door, and trying to sound a great deal braver than she was actually feeling.

"The blood ..." mumbled the stranger in a low and ominous voice. She looked around her as if she were recalling something heinous, her mouth turned down at the corners in disgust.

"How did you get in here?" Marcia asked, staying put in the doorway, sensing that the old woman was not all that she seemed.

The woman barely paid her any attention, but just continued looking around. Then in a low crackly voice she exclaimed, "You should have seen the blood on these walls. Her brains were everywhere."

Marcia backed away into the hall and firmly shut the parlour door. She went out into the front garden and wondered if she should call the police, or maybe an ambulance to remove the confused old woman from the front parlour. Still not sure, she peeped through the parlour window, and found the room completely empty. She was so unnerved by this impossible vanishing act, that she phoned Lindsey and begged her to come over to Prenton to spend a few hours with her. Lindsey could hear the distress in her friend's voice and eventually agreed to travel over to Prenton. She arrived at 11.15pm.

Lindsey listened patiently to Marcia as she reeled off the succession of events that had taken place during the past twenty-four hours. She could see that she was deeply upset, but felt that she must be seeing things, probably because she had been so stressed out by all the rows she had been having with her husband Dave. Marcia was frustrated by her response and vehemently insisted that she had not imagined the strange events in the house, which she was now convinced must be haunted. It was very late and so Lindsey decided to stay overnight. Before she retired for the night she tried her utmost to convince Marcia that there were no such things as ghosts.

"I know what I saw, Lindsey. Real people don't walk through walls and real people don't just disappear."

"Okay, well, we'll talk about it in the morning. I'm off to bed now. I'm shattered. See you tomorrow."

"Night night. I'll be up in a bit. I'm just going to make myself a last cup of coffee to calm my nerves."

At 2am, as Marcia was downstairs in the kitchen, waiting for the kettle to boil, her mobile rang and Lindsey's name came up on the display screen. She grinned, because she knew full well that Lindsey was upstairs in bed. She was probably playing a trick.

But Lindsey was deadly serious. She was making the call from under the bedclothes – because the old woman that Marcia had encountered in the parlour earlier on, was now right there in her bedroom. She sounded absolutely petrified, and pleaded with her friend to come and help at once. Marcia flew up the stairs, two at a time, and into Lindsey's room. On the bed she saw the shapes of two people under the duvet.

The most awful screams came from under those covers, and also a strange hooting laugh. Marcia drew on an inner strength that she never knew she possessed, and pulled down the top of the duvet to reveal a frantic Lindsey curled up in a ball in a dreadful state. Her mascara, mingled with tears, was running in streaks down her cheeks.

"Get her off me! Get her off me!" she screamed, and Marcia dragged the duvet off the bed, expecting to find the old woman – but there was no old woman there. They had both heard her cackling with laughter, and Lindsey had felt the weird white haired crone's fingernails clawing at her skin.

The two women had had enough. Having grabbed their belongings, they quickly jumped into Lindsey's car and drove back to Liverpool, hardly daring to speak about the night's traumatic and inexplicable events. Marcia's mobile phone bleeped just as the car was going into the Queensway Tunnel. She looked at the text message and trembled, because it read: Lindsey Quayle dies tonight.

Of course, it was Lindsey Quayle who was driving Marcia home, and she casually asked her friend who had sent the text. Marcia was so devastated that she couldn't even offer her a proper excuse, but lamely replied, "Er, no one, the battery's just low."

Thankfully, the chilling text prediction did not come to pass and, like the unsettling text message about the death of Kerry Williams, it had no identifying caller number.

Gemma and her family in Spain were furious at their house minder abandoning the job because of some nonsense about ghosts, but weeks after their return from the Costa del Sol, weird things began to unfold in the house which ultimately resulted in the family moving out. Marcia and Lindsey later learned that their friend Kerry had died as a result of an artery in her heart becoming calcified and gone undetected for years. The girl had been found dead in the bath that morning by her husband. He had been in such a state of shock that he had told no one for hours, and yet Marcia had received news of the death by text message within minutes of it occurring.

The identities of the shadowy figures that walk through walls and haunt the house are still unknown. In my files, an unsatisfactory question mark is still scrawled on the folder containing this case.

HALF MAN, HALF WOMAN

In 1968, thirteen-year-old Becky Roberts of Speke was spending the summer holidays with her fifteen-year-old cousin Rosy in Hooton, Wirral. The girls spent the first day together riding a pair of Raleigh bikes through the leafy Cheshire lanes, until the gear-chain of Becky's bike came off near a remote place known as Meadow Bank, close to Thornton Hall. As Rosy was attempting to fix the troublesome chain, a boy dressed in the distinctive gear of a Mod came tootling down Heath Lane on a trendy Lambretta scooter. The lad looked about sixteen, and he slowed, rolled to a halt, and then sat astride his scooter with a fixed expression on his face, as he watched Rosy getting her hands filthy from the gear-chain grease, as she struggled to manoeuvre it back on.

Eventually he asked if he could help, and Rosy smiled and nodded gratefully. The young Mod, resplendent in his up-to-the-minute collar and tie, waist-length leather jacket, tight jeans and ankle-length boots, dismounted and then quickly and effortlessly fixed the gear-chain back on Becky's bike. He introduced himself as Gary Knewel and the girls soon got chatting with him and took turns riding pillion on the scooter, screaming and giggling with excitement. Gary told his two young admirers that he lived in Eastham and admitted that the scooter was not his; he had borrowed it from his older brother just for the day.

By 4pm, having eventually tired of the scooter riding, Becky, Rosy and Gary were loitering on Badgersrake Lane. It had been a gloriously exciting day; the first time either of the girls had had anything to do with a boy, let alone one with a scooter and they were reluctant to say goodbye and return home. All three were looking in the general direction of the railway line, a few hundred yards away, when Rosy suddenly noticed something. A female figure was lying across the track, straight as a mummy, arms by her sides. Gary and Becky soon spotted the suicidal woman as well. Before they had time to think, or decide what action to take, they became conscious of an ominous dull rumble – a train was coming down the track! Gary tore off down the lane on his scooter, shouting, "Stay there!" to the girls.

Within a minute he had reached the grassy slope of the embankment. With the noise of the approaching train thundering in his ears, he hurtled down the slope until he came to a fence, but before he could even attempt to climb it to reach the woman, the train had rattled past. He stood there, rooted to the spot, not knowing what horror would confront him once the train had passed. Yet when the last carriage had sped past in a blur, the carnage he had dreaded seeing did not materialise. There was no trace of the woman on the track, or on either side of the embankment.

Rosy and Becky had also run to the scene and now joined Gary at the fence, all three equally baffled by the miraculous vanishing act. The one inescapable fact was that they had all seen the woman and so they decided that the responsible thing to do was to inform the police of what had happened. Gary, fearful that he was too young to be riding a scooter that was not his, was reluctant to contact the police himself and so he hid behind the cover of a farm building, whilst Rosy went in search of a policeman. She found one walking his beat on Berwick Road, and rather than treat her story with scepticism, as she had feared, he turned pale as she told him what they had just witnessed.

Initially seemingly lost for words, when he had managed to compose himself, he told her to run along home. Rosy reported his strange reaction back to the others, and they went over and over the events of the afternoon, trying to make sense of what they had seen.

An hour later, Gary parted company with the girls and they cycled back towards home. As they passed Sutton Hall, they came across what was obviously a man dressed in women's clothing and a ginger wig, peeping at them over a hedge. Becky was rather unnerved by the sight of the transvestite, but Rosy just laughed at the man's heavy make-up and called him a clown.

That night, Becky slept in the spare room at Rosy's house, and at around 3am she was awakened by a pair of icy hands throttling her. She awoke to see the man in drag whom she had mocked earlier in the day, or strictly speaking, half of the man in drag, because below the waist, his body was missing. Becky screamed from the depths of her lungs, waking the whole household, upon which, the apparition vanished. The truncated intruder left her feeling so traumatised that she refused to go back to sleep and returned home to Liverpool on the following day.

Many years later, Rosy was told a chilling tale by her grandfather, which rekindled memories of that short but eventful holiday in Hooton.

Sometime in the 1950s, a male transvestite had committed suicide by lying on the local railway tracks and waiting for an oncoming train. His body was sliced in two at the waist by the train, and the man's wife and sons, on discovering the body and wishing to avoid a scandal, secretly buried the bisected remains in the garden of their home. To explain her husband's sudden disappearance, the wife claimed, to anyone who asked, that he had left her for a new life, and she even typed a letter stating that fact, which she posted to herself from Chester.

On the evening of the suicide, a sheep from a farm near Childer Thornton was stolen and killed by one of the woman's sons, and the carcass placed on the tracks that evening, to account for the massive pool of blood. The garden of the house in which Becky lived was rumoured to be the resting place of the transvestite's body, and occasionally, over the years, a ghost of the suicide has been seen to emerge from the garden and to float about, minus its legs and thighs and lower abdomen.

Apparently, even several policemen and a railway worker had seen what they assumed to be a woman, lying on the railway track close to Badgersrake Lane, but whenever they hurried to the spot, the woman had vanished. Rosy went cold as her grandfather was telling her all this, and the tale played on her mind to such an extent, that, for the sake of her sanity, she and her family eventually had to move from the house in Hooton and they subsequently settled in Whitby, on the east coast.

They may have escaped, but the house in which Rosy lived is still standing to this day, and I have received occasional reports of ghostly goings-on at the house which lead me to suspect that the phantom transvestite is still on the prowl ...

Haunted Churchyard

Without a doubt, the village church of St Andrews, in Bebington, is haunted and robed figures, resembling monks, have been seen in the grounds of the church many times over the years. The building dates back to Norman times but on the same site, there once stood another church in the Saxon era, built of wood. This long ecclesiastical history of the site may throw some light on the ghostly 'monks' seen gliding through the churchyard, sometimes appearing to be abnormally tall, because they look as if they are walking along an ancient pathway, that is almost two feet above the present ground level, although one woman saw a monk coming towards her in 2001, and he was only visible from the knees upwards, because he was apparently walking on a track that once existed below the level of the churchyard ground. When the apparition came within twenty feet of the startled witness, it slowly dissolved into thin air. These monks have been seen walking from the churchyard to the old collegiate house on Kirket Lane, and some investigators of the paranormal have surmised that the phantoms are the shades of young 'trainee' monks travelling down to Chester, since novices were trained at St Andrew's centuries ago.

A man named Alan, who lives in one of the drives off Kirket Lane, just around the corner from the church, told me how, in the summer of 2007, he was walking his dog one evening when he decided to take a look inside St Andrew's churchyard. The dog started to behave strangely the minute they entered the churchyard. Its ears flew back and it started to crawl along the ground, as if it were afraid of something inside the churchyard. Alan patted the dog and tried to reassure it, then looked round to see what could have panicked it. It was then that he noticed a hooded monk in a grey cowl, standing under a nearby tree. He was more intrigued than afraid of the monk, and watched, fascinated, as the solid-looking ghost intoned something in what sounded like Latin. The monk was obviously the object of the dog's increasing terror and he seemed to suffer a fit, rolling over on his back, eyes bulging and tongue lolling out. Alan picked him up and retreated quickly out of the churchyard, glancing back at the apparition several times and each time he was still standing, stock still, under the tree.

The next day, as the congregation were at Mass in the church, the tree under which the monk had stood suddenly and mysteriously fell down. Whether it was the tree's age (although it didn't seem that old and was perfectly healthy), or the weather (which was calm and pleasant), that made the tree topple, is unknown, but those two causes were cited by the baffled locals who were not aware of a third, supernatural reason for the loss of the tree. Alan's dog continued to behave strangely for several days, and now squarely refuses to be taken anywhere near the churchyard. The ghostly monks of St Andrew's Church are well known and well documented amongst the paranormal community, but Bebington has been at the centre of many other less-known supernatural goings-on.

* * * *

Within a stone's throw of St Andrew's Church is Quarry Road East, which runs from Bromborough Road to Quarry Avenue. At a semi-detached house on Quarry Road East, in the autumn of 2002, a number of strange occurrences took place. In the first, Jane, a woman in her mid-thirties, was having a shower one evening, when she noticed what she presumed to be her teenaged daughter Helena in the bathroom through the steamed up panes of the shower cubicle. "Hey! D'you mind, Helen? I'm getting a shower!" she shouted, but the figure didn't flinch and instead came right up to the shower cubicle. Jane almost fainted with the shock, because the face pressed up against the shower screen was not that of her daughter. This face was as white as chalk, with gaping black eyeless sockets and white hair tied up in a bun. The figure was draped in old fashioned clothes: a long dark green dress with a high collar that went down to the floor.

Jane yelled for her husband Tony, and the figure moved slowly and silently away and seemed to vanish without going out through the door. Tony didn't hear his wife's cries, as he was watching television downstairs, and so Jane burst out of the shower, leaving the water running, grabbed a towel and ran screaming downstairs into the lounge.

It turned out that Jane's seventeen-year-old daughter Helena wasn't even in the house at the time, but was at her friend's on Church Road. Tony knew that his wife didn't even believe in ghosts, and she certainly wasn't the sort to stage a silly practical joke. She must have seen something, because he had never seen her looking so shaken and pale. He wondered if someone might have broken into the house and searched the bedrooms upstairs, but there was no one there – only his thirteen-year-old son Matt playing on his Playstation in his bedroom, oblivious to all the commotion. He had heard nothing, not even his mother's desperate shouts, but that was not unusual when he was in the middle of playing an absorbing game.

On the following evening, at 2am, Jane's ten-year-old daughter Hannah went downstairs to the kitchen to fetch a bottle of mineral water from the fridge. She had been suffering from a week-long cold, which had left her feeling dehydrated. As she passed the doorway to the lounge, on her way back to the stairs, she happened to glance in and saw four people whom she had never seen before, sitting in the dark around the fire. One of these strangers wore her hair up in a bun and had on a long old-fashioned dress. Hannah couldn't make out too many details, because the figures could only be seen in silhouette against the flame-effect gas fire; the rest of the room was in complete darkness. She tiptoed past the door, so as not to alert them to her presence and then scurried up the stairs to her parents' room and woke her mother.

"What's the matter, love? Don't you feel very well?"

" No, mum. They're downstairs ... in front of the fire downstairs ... in the lounge ..." she panted.

"Who's downstairs? What are you ..."

Jane stopped mid-sentence, for she could now hear the hubbub of conversation coming from the living room. She prodded her husband. "Tony! Wake up!" When he had come to his senses she whispered that there were intruders downstairs ... Hannah had seen them. Tony crept downstairs with Jane and Hannah following behind him, and when all three reached the hallway, they looked into the lounge and beheld the most curious sight: no burglars, or people of any sort, just four empty chairs from the dining area, arranged in a semi-circle around the fire, which was still lit. Once again Tony thoroughly searched the house, unable to accept that his home had been the scene of another inexplicable, and therefore possibly supernatural, visitation. Once again, he found no trespassers and no sign of any break-in and he could come up with no rational explanation for what had happened.

Footsteps were heard on the stairs for days afterwards, and in the kitchen the electric kettle began to switch itself on when no one was anywhere near it. Then, some weeks later, on the afternoon of 31 October – Halloween – Hannah left her bedroom and was walking past the toilet when she felt someone place their foot in front of her foot on the landing. She tripped, but quickly scrambled to her feet and watched as the toilet door slowly closed itself.

Then, one late afternoon in December 2002, Jane, Tony and her children had just returned from a shopping trip, when Helena went up to her room to find that it was in total darkness; not a chink of light anywhere. Yes it was a dark December afternoon, but usually the street lights lit up the room. What could have happened? When she turned on the light she immediately realised why the room was so dark – the window panes had been painted black. The paint was later found to be black gloss, and yet it was bone dry, even though the family had only been out of the house for a maximum of forty minutes. The paint had been taken from a cupboard downstairs, and the brush that someone (or something) had used to paint the window panes, was never found. There wasn't even the faintest aroma of wet paint in the room.

Helena was so spooked by this latest incident that her father moved her bed into her younger sister's room and she slept in there until the paint could be laboriously scraped off the window panes – no easy task! by this time, ripples of unease were affecting the entire family. They were all on edge trying to anticipate what might happen next.

In an attempt to lighten the mood in the house, Tony decided that what they needed was a bit of Christmas spirit and to set the ball rolling, he climbed up into the loft to bring down their artificial Christmas tree, and while he was rummaging about up there, he came across a very unusual statue which he did not recognise. One half of the statue represented what looked like a robed saint, complete with halo, but on the other side there was the representation of some horned deity with a goat's head. Tony had been into the loft a few months earlier looking for something and he had not noticed it then.

The instant Tony picked up the odd statue, a cold wind came from nowhere and blasted through the loft, disturbing the blanket of dust which was covering everything. He quickly grabbed the tree and the statue and took them both downstairs to show to Jane. After studying the statue for a short while, she said that she didn't like the look of it; there was something really creepy and not quite right about it.

"Go and throw it in the wheelie bin, Tony, before the kids see it," she said.

"I know what you mean. I don't like the look of it either, but it could be worth a fair bit, you know."

"Maybe, but just get rid of it, please."

"Okay. You're the boss."

And so the schizophrenic statue ended up in the dustbin. After this was done, there were no further spine-chilling incidents in the house on Quarry Road East. Where that double-sided statue came from remains a mystery.

THE FOREST

I see the sunstruck forest,
In green it stands complete,
There soon we will be going,
Our destiny to meet.

Anon

The popular Royal Tiger Club, which once existed on Liverpool's Manchester Street, close to the mouth of the Queensway Tunnel, was frequented mainly by journalists from the nearby *Liverpool Echo* and *Daily Post* offices on Victoria Street and, for some reason, professional footballers, their wives, managers, and occasionally, musicians such as jazz icons Kenny Ball and Acker Bilk. Of course, the clientele also included office workers, because the Tiger was situated in a white-collar district of the city centre, and many a parched clerk would seek alcoholic refreshment at the club before going home.

One evening at the club, in the late summer of 1966, two twenty-four-year-old office workers, Jack from Wallasey and Rod from Walton, were bemoaning their lack of success with the opposite sex, when Jack suddenly remembered having seen Carol, an old flame of Rod's, working alongside her father on the allotments off Claremount Road in Wallasey. Two years before, Rod had dated the beautiful Jean Shrimpton look-alike for just over a month – the best month of his life – and had even asked her to marry him. To his eternal dismay, Carol had turned him down and then moved to Wirral with her family. Soon afterwards he heard that she had started dating a local chef and he knew that he ad to try and forget about her.

Earlier in the year, Jack had obtained a plot on the same allotments where he knew Carol's dad had one, and seeing Rod's reaction when he told him about Carol, he asked him to help harvest his onions on the following Saturday – and, of course, Rod grabbed at the opportunity with both hands. However, when poor Rod drove over to Wirral that Saturday morning, brimful of hope and expectation, little did he realise that, not only was he destined to stay out in the cold as far as Carol was concerned, but also that he was to about receive a nasty shock that would leave a deep and long lasting impression. As he drove his Hillman Imp past the Breck Recreation Ground in Wallasey, he spotted the object of his love walking hand-in-hand with a tall well-dressed young man. With a heavy heart and his hopes dashed, he proceeded towards the allotments.

That sunny afternoon, Jack and Rod pottered about on the plot for a while, harvesting the onions and doing a bit of weeding, but Jack could see that Rod was struggling with his emotions and suggested going for a walk along the coast at King's Parade. It was a decision which landed them in the thick of a mystery that remains unsolved to this day. When they reached the parade, instead of the clear panorama of Liverpool Bay which they had been expecting, their view was obscured by an extraordinarily flattened white cloud lying just above the waters, stretching from Mockbeggar Wharf as far as the eye could see. Several other people were gazing at this meteorological mystery from the vantage point of the parade, but Jack and Rod wanted to get closer and jumped down on to the sands to get a better look. Through the misty folds of the cloud they saw an incredible sight: a vast forest, stretching out to sea as far as the eye could see. It seemed impossible, yet there it was, as plain as day.

Rod hurried towards the sylvan green mirage, despite Jack's caution to keep well clear of it. The Waltonian waded knee-deep through the water for some seventy feet or so before he found himself beneath the towering trees. He continued on, trudging across a forest floor carpeted with oversized ferns, exotic orchids of every shape and colour and damp spongy mosses. Through the sweet-smelling mists, Rod could make out the bulbous forms of enormous speckled toadstools jutting out from the roots of trees that were taller and whose trunks were thicker than Liverpool's Wellington's Column. Ahead of him a huge butterfly, the size of a small kite, with silken wings of electric blue with black and white markings, fluttered about in a ray of bright sunlight which had managed to penetrate the thick canopy.

Jack, meanwhile, was looking away from the impossible forest towards the Coastguard Lookout post at the end of King's Parade; surely the guard couldn't fail to have noticed this colossal spectacle?

"Jack! Look at this!" bellowed Rod, pointing at something out of sight in the depths of the forest, as he frantically splashed his way back through the water towards his cautious friend with a look of terror etched on his face. "Run!" he screamed, and bolted back up the beach past Jack. A thunderous chorus of fearsome roars reverberated through the forest, as if a pride of lions was pounding through the undergrowth. Jack felt the breath leave his body as his lungs were seized with panic and he ran stumbling up the beach, sweating profusely – but he was too slow and the beasts were soon upon him!

Three fear-inspiring creatures, resembling lions but twice their length, came bounding out of the forest at lightning speed. Jack desperately tried to make his escape, but the soft sand gave way under his feet and his body would not respond to his commands, so overcome was he with fear. The collective deep growls as the creatures bore down on him vibrated through every nerve and fibre of his body. He screwed his eyes shut, ready to die. As he did so he became aware of a powerful icy wind blowing straight through him from behind. The snarling sounds then moved ahead of him and grew fainter, and when he dared to open his eyes once more, he saw the fresh tracks of the now invisible beasts in the wet sand ahead of him. The imprints of three sets of huge paws, each a foot in diameter, were all that remained in a trail that petered out to nothing in the sand some thirty feet away.

Once the fiendish cats had disappeared, Rod then came running back to help his friend.

"Are you okay?" he panted.

Jack swore at him for running off, "Yeah, I think so, but no thanks to you. Some mate you are!"

But Rod ignored the rebuke and merely pointed to the cloud forest hovering above the sea and said, "It's going. Look! I think it's going."

The whole mirage, vision, or whatever it was, slowly dissipated as the two men looked on, and within just a few seconds it was gone, along with the bizarre sea-level cloud which had enshrouded it. The two men stood there, stupefied, unable to do anything but shake their heads in disbelief.

"I thought I was a gonner back there," said Jack eventually.

"Me too! What on earth was all that about? I've never seen anything like it in my life."

"Yeah ... those trees ... and those bloomin' great lions, or panthers, or whatever they were ... and now they've gone, thank god! If I'd have been on my own I'd have thought I'd been seeing things."

"I know what you mean … but things can't just vanish, can they? It was all so real."

"You're not kidding! You should have come into the forest. Honest to god, it was like being in that telly programme where they're all in the middle of the jungle."

The two men talked about nothing else for the rest of the day, going over every detail again and again in an attempt to make sense of their experiences. In fact, so fascinated were they, that despite their fear, almost every Saturday in the ensuing months Jack and Rod felt compelled to return to King's Parade and to stare out into Liverpool Bay, waiting to see if the perilous phantom forest would appear once more, but so far it has not materialised.

Then one day, in 1967, an old vagrant came up to the two men as they stood gazing out across the waters, and with a toothless grin told them how he had watched the "peculiar goings-on" that day last summer. The tramp claimed to have seen the forest appear and then disappear three times in all, and on one occasion, late at night, he said he had seen "a cat as big as a horse" prowling about along the moonlit shore, not far from a love-struck courting couple who were blissfully oblivious to its presence.

Rod was still looking for explanations and so he wrote an account of his and Jack's extraordinary experiences and emailed it to me a few years ago. After some research I discovered that some two thousand years before the birth of Christ, a great forest stretched from Crosby, right across the mouth of the Mersey to New Brighton and Leasowe. At unusually low tides at Hightown and Leasowe, the withered stumps of trees from this long-forgotten forest have been reported on many occasions. I firmly believe that Jack, Rod, the unknown vagrant, and many more people besides, have seen this ancient forest, not as it is now, but as it used to be, literally through the mists of time, by way of what we would normally term a timeslip. Thousands of years ago, it was possible to walk from Wirral to Crosby via this forest that stretched across the estuary of the Mersey. So what happened to that green tract? Some think colossal glaciers of a bygone Ice Age may have cut through it, but no one knows for sure.

In 2005, a man named Paul wrote to me, telling how, in August 1964, when he was twenty-one, he went to visit an elderly aunt at a rest home on St Hilary Drive in Wallasey. The home was hot and stuffy and so after the visit, Paul and his friend Alf went to buy ice creams before taking a refreshing walk along King's Drive. They, and at least a dozen other people, watched as the mirage of a distinctive leafy forest slowly materialised on the waters, about one hundred yards from Mockbeggar Wharf. Paul noticed that the trees were incredibly tall, and he also heard loud chirps from birds somewhere within the mirage. A minute later the forest had faded away to leave an unsettling stillness in the air. Paul's friend Alf had been so mesmerised by the entire spectral display, that he hadn't noticed that his ice cream had fallen out of its cone!

If the remote past does indeed sometimes intrude into the present day, then it would certainly explain cryptozoological anomalies such as the Loch Ness monster, which may turn out to be some time-displaced aquatic dinosaur. The Surrey Puma, Beast of Exmoor, and other baffling 'big cats' which have been seen the length and breadth of the country, could also be explained by this timeslip hypothesis.

Bidston Hill, one of the highest points on Wirral, has long been regarded as the gateway to another world (in the mystical sense), and from the many reports of supernatural goings on there, I would agree that there is almost certainly a time portal somewhere amid the hundred acres of heathland that cover the hill. I have personally received so many reports of timeslips and inexplicable time loss on Bidston Hill and here is just one of them.

* * * *

Throughout August 2003, several people contacted me by email and snail mail to relate sightings of a huge cat with prominent 'tusks' of some sort that had been seen slinking around on Bidston Hill. Disturbingly, the reports fitted the description of the long-vanished sabre-toothed tiger which lived between 2.5 million and 10,000 years ago. A Wildlife Liaison Officer for Merseyside Police even looked into one sighting of the mysterious 'Bidston Big Cat' in August 2003 but drew a blank.

In the 1960s, there was a spate of alleged wolf encounters on Bidston Hill, often occurring in conjunction with the appearance of a long-haired individual whose dress resembled that of a peasant from the Middle Ages. Sometimes the wolf was seen running alongside this anachronistic walker on the hill, and on one occasion a woman out taking her dog for a morning stroll was attacked by the wolf. The outdated-looking man, on seeing her predicament, shouted something at the wolf, which immediately loped over to him. Soon afterwards, the wolf and the oddly dressed stranger vanished as they came close to Bidston Hill windmill.

Of course, in this country, the wolf became extinct during the reign of Henry VII (1485-1509), so we must either conclude that the scores of witnesses of this phenomenon either mistook a large alsation, or similar large dog, for a wolf, or that the fifteenth and sixteenth centuries often overlap our present time.

THE MOON DANCER OMEN

"Not only is the universe far stranger than we imagine, it is stranger than we can ever imagine," English astrophysicist Sir Arthur Eddington once remarked, and after studying the supernatural for many years, I would argue that, if anything, that is an understatement. Beneath the tides of time and space, very strange fish are swimming. Over the years, readers of my books and newspaper columns, as well as listeners to my radio broadcasts, have related some very strange and eerie tales to me, and sometimes their stories dovetail together, which gives the unearthly accounts a far greater measure of credibility. This has certainly been the case with the Dancing Man Death Omen, an extraordinary and chilling phenomenon seen mainly from the Wirral, but also in some parts of Liverpool and Wales.

On the Saturday evening of 24 January 1959, when a full moon hung low in the sky, two Teddy Boys drinking in the Coffee House pub in Liverpool's Wavertree district simultaneously put down their pints. They had both spotted something very strange indeed in the night sky which could be seen through the pub window. A small fluffy cloud was obscuring the base of the lunar disk, and on the cloud's convoluted surface there stood the distinctive silhouette of a man, and he appeared to be dancing.

The Teds excitedly pointed out this uncanny sight to the other drinkers present, and within minutes a moon-gazing crowd had assembled outside the pub. Some tried to dismiss the dancing shadow as a trick of the light, but it was plain to see that it was nothing of the sort – it was definitely some gravity-defying person – although just what he was doing up there they couldn't imagine. A retired seaman named

Brogan then produced a brass three-fold pocket telescope and trained it on the cloud dancer. As soon as the former sailor had managed to bring the figure into focus, his expression changed and he gravely declared that they were looking at the Devil himself. One of the Teds then rudely wrestled the spyglass from Brogan's hands and squinted through it with his own eyes. The hushed crowd waited with bated breath for his verdict on the apparition. There was definitely someone up there, he said, and he was "dancing like a madman".

After ten minutes or so, the cloud slowly slid away from the moon, and as it did so, the apparition vanished too. Some of the more superstitious amongst them feared that the silhouetted sky performer was some kind of omen of a forthcoming tragedy, and when Buddy Holly died in a plane crash just over a week later, a few of the drinkers in the Coffee House were mindful of the weird figure on the cloud but kept it to themselves.

Ten years afterwards, on the night of Thursday, 3 July 1969, the Dancing Man was back on his cloud, silhouetted in front of a waning gibbous moon. This time he was seen not just over Wavertree, but in places ranging from Kensington to Heswall, with most of the sightings coming from Wirral. Terry Moore, one of the Teddy Boys who had seen the strange silhouette a decade before in the Coffee House, in Wavertree, experienced a sense of déjà vu as he walked up Birkenhead's Grange Road arm in arm with his fiancée. He squinted skywards in disbelief at the eerily familiar dark outline of the dancing man, standing out clearly against the moon. His girlfriend also saw the figure, and finding the sight very creepy, urged Terry to take her straight home.

Over on New Chester Road in New Ferry, something

moving in a cloud attracted the attention of two men walking past St Mark's vicarage. The men looked up to see strange shadows flitting about in a moonlit cloud, but couldn't see what was casting them. Checking the date of these sightings, to see if the unearthly wingless angel was perhaps (as some believed) a harbinger of death, it was intriguing to discover that Brian Jones, of the Rolling Stones, died that very night, after taking a midnight dip in his swimming pool in the grounds of his luxurious Sussex home. The coroner's report recorded a verdict of 'death by misadventure' and an autopsy revealed that the rock musician's heart and liver were grossly enlarged as a result of drug and alcohol abuse.

There were sightings of the sinister cloud-dancer in the August and September of 1977 – the months in which Elvis and Marc Bolan died. I have received two further reports of the nocturnal nimble-footed nimbus-cloud dweller engaged in his 'danse macabre'.

On Monday, 24 November 1980, at around 10.30pm, a woman in Caldy saw something "wriggling" on a cloud in front of the moon, but having rather weak long distance vision, she couldn't see the object as clearly as she would have liked. However, on the other side of the Mersey, a security guard standing outside a Kirkby factory, who had 20/20 vision, got a very good view of the phantasm that night. The guard telephoned his mother in Northwood, and she and several of her neighbours also saw the mysterious dancer. A fortnight later, John Lennon was killed in New York.

The apparition was last seen sometime in late January 1983, and it may be just a dark coincidence, but another rock musician died that month, and a local one at that. Billy Fury sadly passed away from a heart problem, which stemmed from the bouts of rheumatic fever which had plagued him from an early age. This last known sighting of the ominous lunar mirage took place on Manor Road, Wallasey, and the witness was a woman named Joanne Wheeler, who was then twenty-seven years of age. She had just visited her mother in Liscard and was walking eastwards, and homewards, up Manor Road, around 11.20pm, when she happened to glance up at the waning moon. For a moment she thought an owl or some other nocturnal bird was flapping its wings in front of the moon, and then she realised that it was not a bird at all, but had a humanoid outline. The figure, a featureless black silhouette, the same as all the other sightings, appeared to be running on the spot and as it moved it swung its bent arms back and forth. When Joanne reached her home on Penkett Road at around 11.30pm, the baleful bopping black figure was still there, but when she woke her husband, and he groggily looked out of the window, he saw nothing but the moon partly obscured now by clouds. Throughout the night, Joanne left her bed to steal a glance at the moon in the hope of catching a glimpse of the dancing man once again, but she saw nothing.

What are we to make of these eldritch sightings of the dancing black figure? Had there been further sightings we could have established the altitude and true position of the apparition by a simple process of triangulation. In an edition of the *Liverpool Mercury*, dated 16 June 1815, there is a report of a similar mirage-like person, seen with some clarity, by one Captain Hayes and his crew on board the *Majestic*, whilst sailing off the coast of Boston. This time against the disk of the rising sun, the figure which materialised was that of a man dressed in a short jacket, with a staff in his hand, on the top of which was a French flag.

This same enigmatic figure was seen over the course of several mornings, both by the naked eye and through a telescope, and was interpreted by some of the superstitious crew as a providential warning of some sort. Had the sun been shining from behind the observer, the 'Broken Spectre' effect would have provided a ready explanation for the mirage, but Captain Hayes and his men reported unequivocally that they were looking into the rising sun, which was directly in front of them.

The skies over Wirral are no strangers to airborne mirages. In the 1930s, for example, there were numerous sightings of a huge white angelic being with enormous wings flying over Wallasey. At around the same time, there was a plethora of reports of a similar angel over the Fazakerley district of Liverpool. A group of children playing near Delagoa Road saw the angel at close quarters, and ran at breakneck speed all the way home, in order to get away from it. One young girl described the unearthly visitor as a bright golden light with two outstretched wings and the outline of a body, hovering about six feet off the ground. She sensed that the angel was friendly, and only ran away because her older brother and friends had already run off in panic.

In 1938, Welshman William Davies, along with several other people, witnessed a disconcerting portent in the sky over the Eastham Ferry Hotel – a shimmering golden swastika. The crooked cross symbol that the world has come to associate exclusively with the Nazis, can, in fact, be traced back to Neolithic times, and can also be found as a sacred symbol used by Hindus, Buddhists, followers of Jainism and Mithraism. The significance of the swastika vision of the Eastham Ferry Hotel is unknown, but within twelve months, of course, the world was plunged into an unprecedented global war by Adolf Hitler, a man whose evil reign was symbolised by the crooked cross emblem that he and all his followers always wore on their arms.

Was the weird dancing shadow of the moonlit Merseyside skies merely a figment of the human imagination, or was it real? Our minds seem to be hard-wired to recognise human shapes in anything from a cloud to a potato, and even upon the face of our ancient satellite world, for has not every culture on this earth imagined a Man in the Moon, from Norway to China, from Australia to America?

This phenomenon is known as 'pareidolia' – a psychological illusion in which we see human forms or faces in random aspects of an image. Somehow, though, I cannot believe that pareidolia is responsible for the sightings of the menacing man in black perched on the silver-lined clouds of the moonlit sky. Perhaps there is some Cosmic Joker up there with a warped sense of humour. In the meantime, before the truth is properly unravelled, keep an eye on the moon, you never know what you might see!

DEADLY ON THE DEE

The River Dee, so ancient legend has it, being a holy river, can never keep a corpse for very long. Late one sunny afternoon, in 1965, twelve-year-old Darren MacEneany was idly looking out of the open attic window of his Uncle Robert's house, situated on the coast between Caldy and Thurstaston. Darren lifted a pair of old brass leather-grip binoculars that his uncle used for bird-watching and surveyed the River Dee looking for boats. Something caught his eye and his binoculars came to rest on an object floating in the middle of the river. Bobbing along on the gold and silver mirrored waves was a dark box of some sort. Having brought it into sharp focus, Darren traced its progress for a while, then, seeing that it was drifting towards the shore, ran downstairs to tell his uncle what he had seen.

Within five minutes, the sixty-year-old man and his excited nephew had run down on the shoreline, and were squinting out to the waters beyond Gayton Sands. The sun's glare, reflected off the river, dazzled their eyes and made it difficult to spot the mysterious object, especially since a sharp wind had begun to whip up from the mouth of the estuary, breaking up the surface into small choppy waves. Then Uncle Robert caught a glimpse of the box being dragged in by the tide, and he and Darren trudged through the sucking sands to take a closer look at the mysterious piece of flotsam.

The box turned out to be a coffin made of dark wood, possibly mahogany and was bound in rusted chains which weighed it down low in the water. It floated slowly in on the incoming tide and was strewn with seaweed, and encrusted with a thick coat of barnacles, which, to young Darren, looked like clusters of sleeping lizards' eyes. Uncle Robert waded out to the coffin with the foamy waters lapping round his boots, and noted the absence of a brass identification plate on the coffin.

"Come away now, Darren," said Uncle Robert, turning away from the washed-up casket and gently tugging at his nephew's upper arm as he shepherded him back up the shore and away from the coffin.

"Whose coffin is it, uncle?" asked Darren nervously, sensing the disquiet his relative was feeling. He reluctantly walked backwards a few feet, but could not take his eyes off the bobbing coffin.

"I said come away!" repeated Robert sternly, this time with a good deal more authority in his voice. "Follow me. We're going back to the house."

"But, uncle ..."

"No buts. Just do as you're told."

"Okay, uncle ... I'm coming," mumbled Darren, sulkily.

He was reluctant to leave the coffin without having investigated it properly. He had just taken a couple of begrudging steps towards his uncle, when the dark sweeping shadow of a low cloud crawled over the sands enveloping him and chilling him to the marrow. He sensed real menace in it and quickly caught up with his uncle.

Not until he saw old Mrs Tollet on Station Road did Robert Dunnachie utter a single word and then he simply returned the aged widow's greeting by uttering a civil, "Good afternoon" and then moved swiftly on. When he reached the path leading to his house, 'White Croft', he suddenly rounded on his nephew and with an uncharacteristically serious expression, started to tell him a tale that would give him horrendous nightmares that night.

It was probably rather irresponsible of him to have imparted the eerie story, perhaps forgetting that his nephew was only twelve years old, but he had always had a habit of imagining Darren to be older than he was.

As they went into the house, the lad listened, fascinated, as Robert revealed that he had heard an old legend at his mother's knee, many decades ago, concerning the restless soul of a Wirral captain by the name of Wode, who had been buried in the Irish Sea in Victorian times. His curiosity was being satisfied at last, and Darren listened to the story without interruption as his uncle turned his back on him to prod the coal fire with a long blackened brass-handled poker.

"A dying man's question must always be answered truthfully, or his soul will never rest," Robert began, solemnly, as Darren sat curled up in the fireside armchair, all eyes and ears. "Captain Wode became ill with a high fever, and was soon at death's door, as his ship ploughed her way across the Atlantic. Minutes before he died, in the arms of his wife, who had accompanied him on what turned out to be his last voyage, he asked her if she had really, truthfully loved him. She began to cry, but gave no answer. 'Answer me,' the dying captain pleaded, 'or my soul shall roam this world for eternity, forever seeking the answer to my question.'

"But Wode's wife was not prepared to admit that she had been unfaithful to her husband, and the captain died in her arms, his fervent request unanswered. He was buried at sea ... because that was the tradition for all sailors who died in the middle of a voyage ... just as the ship entered the Irish Sea, and that should have been the end of the story."

For several minutes Uncle Robert sat in his odd-looking three-legged elm corner chair, scratching the clump of grey hair on the left side of his bald pate, without saying a word. Darren was desperate to hear what happened next but he had the sense to see that his uncle was struggling to find a way to continue.

Eventually, Robert took a deep breath and resumed his woeful tale. He described how, on the Christmas Eve after Wode had been committed to the deep, a coffin, bound in heavy chains, was washed ashore one morning at Caldy Blacks mussel bed. Not one of the superstitious locals dared to even touch the coffin and so it lay there for a full twelve hours, being gently lapped by the river, whilst the gossiping villagers looked on from what they considered to be a safe distance.

Even when night fell, there was still a fair-sized crowd staring at the mysterious coffin, all exchanging anxious whispers. Who knows what they were expecting to happen, but when the coffin began to rock, gently at first, and then more violently, until the lid became loose, the startled onlookers stopped their whispering and watched in disbelief. Suddenly, the lid flew open and the chains fell away, as the grotesque decaying form of Captain Wode, rose up and started walking towards Shore Cottages, in search of his unfaithful wife. As he walked, his rotting feet left a trail of slime in the sand.

Mrs Wode unwittingly opened her front door to be confronted by the dripping corpse of her late husband, upon whose still discernible features there was a quizzical look. The late captain's wife slammed the door shut but could still hear the captain's skeletal hands scratching at the wood. The experience rendered her mute with shock and she hastily packed a bag and decamped overnight to Chester, but the accusing image of her dead husband went with her inside her head. She was quite unable to recover from the trauma of what she had seen that night, and she died a year later.

They say that the captain had dabbled in West African Voodoo magic during his lifetime, and had sold his soul to the Devil in exchange for a guarantee that his business would prosper, so perhaps this also had something to do with his ghastly reappearances.

"And now," sighed Robert Dunnachie, pausing to increase the dramatic effect on his nephew, "every thirteen years, Captain Wode's coffin returns from the underwater domain of the drowned ... known to mortals as Davy Jones' Locker ... to the coastline of his home."

Young Darren had sat through the whole story completely enthralled. "Do you think that was his coffin we saw today?" he asked, his heart in his mouth.

"Aye, lad. I do. And what's more, the reason I didn't want you meddling with it, is that there's a belief hereabouts ... well, let's just say that people think that anyone who happens to see Wode's face ... accidentally or not ... will be struck down ... just like poor Mrs Wode."

"You mean killed?"

"All I'm saying is that we don't want anything to do with that horrible coffin, understand? Let's just hope the tide takes it back out tonight."

"Flippin' eck!" said Darren. "Wait till I tell me mates all this."

"Anyway, Darren, look at the time! It's way past your bedtime. Off you go to bed now, and as they say on that *Crimewatch* programme, Don't have nightmares!"

At one o'clock in the morning, young Darren woke in his bedroom, gasping for air. He had suffered a harrowing nightmare in which Captain Wode's rattling skeleton had chased him along the beach. Diffused moonlight passing through the net curtains paled the bed covers, and the boy lay there with his heart pulsating, relieved that it was all a bad dream. The fear eventually evaporated from Darren's mind, and he went to the window to part the net curtains.

"They say that death strikes the person who see's the dead captain's face," came a voice from inside his head. It was his uncle's voice and the message made him shudder.

Not surprisingly, he could not get back to sleep that night, and when the reassuring glow of dawn shone from behind the house, the boy decided to go looking for a thrill – and a very dangerous one at that. He silently dressed and crept downstairs in his bare feet. A couple of the stairs creaked very loudly and he stopped, listening out for his uncle, but all he could hear were faint snores coming from his room. The key to the front door was in the lock and he sneaked out of the house without being caught and sat on the step whilst he put on his shoes. He then made his way to the shoreline – his daring mission, to check if the coffin was still there.

On the way he bumped into the harmless local vagrant, Mr Keyhoe, and his little black and white mongrel dog, Tanner. Keyhoe was drunk as usual, but typically mellow and giggly, and Tanner wagged its tail as it trotted towards Darren for a stroke. In a conspiratorial whisper he told the elderly tramp about the coffin on the beach, which information instantly wiped the inane smile off Keyhoe's face. He began to sway backwards and forwards in the most alarming manner, and seemed extremely edgy all of a sudden. Darren told Keyhoe not to worry, because the sun had just risen, and the coffin was most probably far out to sea by now.

Then, all of a sudden, an elongated early morning shadow appeared in the sand alongside Darren. Before he had a chance to turn and see who was casting the shadow, Keyhoe's eyes bulged and his face twisted in anguish and Tanner pointed his little grey muzzle to the skies and howled pitifully. Keyhoe collapsed on to his knees, then fell face first into the sand. At the same time, Tanner rolled over on to his side and started foaming at the mouth, before falling silent.

Darren knew only too well that Captain Wode was behind him, and all his basic instincts screamed at him to run, but his legs felt numb, heavy and useless. He could hear the scrunching sound of footsteps in the sand behind him, and saw Wode's shadow coinciding with his own.

"Uncle!" he shouted, "Uncle help me, please!"

Just as the shadow was upon him, he suddenly regained the power of movement in his legs and started running for his life. He was so petrified of being struck down by the deathly gaze of the returned sea captain's face, that he rushed blindly towards the sea. As he neared the water's edge, he veered off to the right – and almost tripped over the gaping coffin of the moribund mariner. The rest was just a blur. He remembered seeing the imprints of a man's feet trailing away from the open coffin, and caught sight fleetingly, from the corner of his eye, a thin tall man in a long black coat.

The death of the drunken vagrant was later put down to natural causes, and some believed that Keyhoe's dog had pined to death after the demise of its master (although pining usually takes a lot longer and Tanner's death happened at virtually the same time as his master's). Of course, Darren knew full well that both man and dog had almost certainly been killed by the lethal gaze of Captain Wode.

Later that day a search of the beach was made for the coffin, but it was nowhere to be found.

It is said that, thirteen years after this sinister incident, a man who was playing golf at Caldy on the links overlooking the coast, was found dead one evening after being seen looking at a mysterious figure on the shore through a pair of binoculars. That same evening, a group of children playing on the dismantled railway tracks saw a long black box on the shoreline. All this could be nothing more than coincidence and mere folklore, of course ...

THE UNSEEN

A ghost that can be seen is bad enough, but how about entities that can only be heard? In one such case, throughout several nights in the summer of 1973, a Mr Thompson, who was working on the Mersey ferries, often heard the unmistakable sound of a woman's high heels clicking into the booking hall at Seacombe Ferry Terminal, with no corresponding female body to accompany them. He still recalls those eerie footsteps to this day, and is convinced that they belonged to a genuine ghost, but exactly whose ghost it was, has yet to be discovered.

Sometimes the click-clacking of the stilettos would speed up as they made their way across the concourse, as though the invisible woman was worried that she was going to miss her ferry. However, not once did Thompson, or any of his co-workers, set eyes on the owner of the high heels.

For many years I have received reports from different people of phantom footsteps and strange goings-on in Church Road, in Higher Tranmere, and one of these reports resulted in a rare and spectacular occurrence – a manifestation of such a ghost – or to be more accurate, a partial materialisation of a violent entity, who behaved like a common street thug.

The first account comes from Theresa, who was just sixteen when this incident took place, in 1965, on a dark foggy November afternoon at around 4 o'clock. Theresa was on her way to the Sweet Lavender Laundrette, on Church Road, carrying a bundle of her grandmother's clothes and as she passed Flynn's the Chemist, someone powerful, but unseen, bashed into her, knocking her to the ground. The invisible attacker then roughly snatched the laundry sack from her hands and flung it down on to the pavement, spilling items of her gran's laundry everywhere.

An old woman called Mrs Lloyd witnessed this bizarre sequence of events, and even heard a loud grunt and heavy footfalls as the entity thumped past her after the attack. After instinctively making the sign of the cross, she ran to check that Theresa was alright, along with another passer-by. They helped her to her feet and collected up all the bits of laundry.

Theresa was very badly shaken up by the incident, but was more confused than afraid. She tried to rationalise what had just taken place – but could come up with no plausible explanation, because there was nothing in her experience with which to compare it. She was certain that it was a man who had collided with her, partly because of the force he exerted, but also because he gave off a sense of maleness. She also recalled that he had given off a ghastly aroma of stale tobacco.

After dusting herself off, she bravely continued on her way to the laundrette, where she loaded her gran's stuff into the washing machine and slotted in the necessary coins to set it going. Only then did she sit down on a bench and try and take stock of what had happened, as she stared at the clothes tumbling round and round in the drum. She knew that she hadn't just tripped – she had felt the bump, and a violent one at that – and was certain that it had been deliberate. Besides, the old woman had seen the whole thing and had also heard what she heard. The only conclusion she could come to, was that she had been harassed by an invisible ghost – something which made her feel very uncomfortable. She picked up a magazine and tried to drive the eerie incident to the back of her mind.

The laundry washed and dried and folded, Theresa left the laundrette and stepped out once again into the fogbound street. She felt herself stiffen as she passed the chemist's and once again heard the slow and determined plodding of the phantom pedestrian. She spun round, determined not to be caught out again, and saw a person-shaped hole in the fog, as clear as if it had been cut out with a stencil. The vapours swirled around the sharp outline of a man of about six feet or more. The entire 'body' was a just cavity of shadows, but it had a kind of depth and was moving rapidly towards Theresa through the fog. She howled with fright and ran like the wind until she reached her grandmother's house, by which time she was exhausted and almost incoherent.

The creepy events of that day were etched on her mind and would come back as flashbacks during the day and as nightmares during sleep. Much as she loved her grandmother and wanted to help her, she did not volunteer to go to the laundrette on Church Road until the summer of the following year.

❋ ❋ ❋ ❋

In the very same month – November 1965 – that Theresa had her encounter with the invisible ghost, a man came out of the Midland Bank on Church Road, and felt someone roughly slam him up against a wall. The fog was thick that day too, with visibility down to no more than twenty metres, but the man could see that no one had passed him, although he did hear footsteps running away. He recalls the date of the assault for two reasons: firstly it was 5 November – Guy Fawkes Night – and it was also the date on which forty-five vehicles crashed in a lethal pile-up on the fogbound M6, which resulted in an inferno. The carnage that day, saw four people dead and many more injured. One fifty-two-year-old motorist, Edward Bynon from Liverpool, in a desperate attempt to leap clear of the crashing cars, had jumped off the motorway flyover, but died after hitting the roadway thirty feet below.

In an even weirder incident, thirty years later, in 1995, seventeen-year-old Martin set off on a mission to spray the name of the football team he supported on to the wall of St Catherine's Church, on Church Road. At around 11pm, the graffiti artist had arrived at the church and, after looking furtively about to check that the coast was clear, shook his can of aerosol paint, and was about to spray the wall, when something stopped him in his tracks. A pair of large disembodied hands shot out of the wall and seized him by the throat. The teenager assumed that the hands had emerged from some hole in the wall that he had overlooked, but as he wrestled to free the ice-cold fingers from his throat, he could see that they protruded from solid brick.

He had almost choked into unconsciousness, when, just as everything was beginning to go dark, he made one last desperate attempt to free himself. Lodging one foot against the wall, he pushed himself backwards with all his might, eventually forcing the hands to let go.

The youth fell heavily on to the path on his back, further knocking the breath out of him. He was so badly winded that it took a couple of minutes before he could manage to scramble to his feet. All thoughts of employing his illegal artistic skills had gone, and casting his spray can into some bushes, he made off down Church Road, his chest still feeling as if it were in a vice, for what seemed like an eternity. When he arrived home, his mother was horrified to see the two massive, angry-looking bruises encircling his throat, just under his adam's apple.

"What on earth's happened to you, Martin?" she cried. "Has someone attacked you on the way home?"

"Honestly, mum," he answered, not wishing to admit that he had been about to graffiti the church wall, "you really don't want to know …"

The next night, Martin took two sceptical friends of his to the church wall where the throttling hands had emerged, and although the hands failed to appear, all three lads heard phantom footsteps coming their way from the church, and they didn't hang around to investigate!

Phantom Cannon Shots

The one o'clock gun was an enormous cannon situated at Morpeth Pier, in Birkenhead. The barrel of the cannon pointed outwards over the River Mersey and provided an important time signal for the shipping trade for many years. Another time signal from Bidston Observatory used to electrically trigger the gun each day at precisely one o'clock. Obviously the cannon did not fire a real projectile, but a blank, which consisted of several pounds of cordite.

This famous time signal was fired for the final time at one o'clock on 20 July 1969. However, since the early 1970s, there have been numerous reports of a loud shot still being heard in the vicinity of Morpeth Dock. For instance, in 1972, at precisely one o'clock in the afternoon, police were called to investigate the source of a loud bang that seemed to be coming from Birkenhead's Bridge Street. The sound was heard and reported by many people in the area, many of whom surmised that the old gun had been fired once again. However, the police checked up and found that the gun had not been discharged. No explanation for the boom was confirmed.

In July 1974, again at one o'clock in the afternoon, scores of people in Birkenhead heard a tremendous explosion, which echoed across the River Mersey. The source of the sound was never determined, but was heard again on three more occasions.

Then, on the night of 6 August 1978, another mysterious explosion, this time of a far greater magnitude, was heard all over Merseyside and the surrounding counties – within a ten mile radius, in fact. *The Liverpool Echo* reported the incident and described how the ground shook all over the region when the mystery explosion was heard. People came forward to describe the effects of the mysterious blast, which included the wardrobe mirror of a house in Liverpool's Lee Park being split in two by the tremor, as well as veranda doors at a house in Crosby being thrown open with the blast.

To explain the immense sound, a sonic boom from Concorde was blamed, but the supersonic airliners were all on the ground at the time. Oil companies drilling in Liverpool Bay were also investigated as a possible cause, but it was found that they were not to blame either and whatever rocked Merseyside that day was never identified.

Strangely enough, a second so-called 'sky quake' was heard during the daytime later that year.

EVIL ASSAILANT

The following chilling story is taken from the annals of the now-defunct Lancashire Spiritualists Society which was based in West Derby, Liverpool, at the turn of the century.

There is a certain Victorian house in Bidston, on the Wirral, which was once the scene of a disturbing supernatural incident that allegedly occurred in 1920. The house was bought by two sisters, Victoria and Margaret Webster, who had been left a substantial legacy in 1919. At the time, Margaret was only nineteen and Victoria twenty-four. They originally came from Neston but moved to the beautiful terraced house in Bidston after the death of their father, a wealthy shipping magnate who had left his daughters a small fortune. Mrs Webster had died after giving birth to Margaret in 1901.

The Webster sisters soon settled into their new home and found the neighbours quite agreeable. Both sisters were said to be very attractive and soon caught the attention of a number of men in their new neighbourhood.

One night, early in December 1920, Victoria was escorted into town by a local government clerk called William. She had been stepping out with him for three months and he was very much in love with her. Margaret had stayed at home and was reading a book. Around midnight, Victoria still hadn't returned, so Margaret went to bed, where she continued reading her book by the light of a candle. She was starting to doze off, when she thought she heard a noise downstairs. Assuming it was her sister, she got up and went to the landing, from where she shouted down the stairs, "Is that you, Victoria?"

No reply came, but Margaret saw a shadowy figure flit

across the bottom flight of stairs and heard a faint chuckle. Probably William teasing Victoria, thought Margaret with a smile. She liked William very much; he made her laugh with his foolish games, so she put on her dressing gown and went downstairs, carrying the candle, expecting to see him staging some prank or other.

As she reached the bottom flight of stairs, she saw the flickering flames of the coal fire still burning in the grate. She had forgotten to put the safety guard around the fire, and as she walked into the parlour to rectify matters, she noticed a figure standing in the shadows of the hallway to her left. It wasn't William, but a stranger, just standing there. He wore a long curly white wig, such as the ones worn by judges and a long embroidered satin coat with large turned-up sleeves, an exact replica of the type of coat worn in the eighteenth century. Beneath this, the stranger wore a silvery waistcoat and instead of trousers, he had on outdated breeches, cut off at the knees. On the lower parts of his legs, he wore white stockings and on his feet were square-toed shoes with shiny buckles. What really spooked young Margaret was the intruder's face, which was thickly plastered with white make-up. He and the terrified girl studied one another for a split second without moving, then he rushed towards her, his face the picture of evil.

Margaret dropped the candlestick and dashed into the parlour, slamming the door behind her and leaning against it with her heart pounding. The intruder started to steadily force the door open, finally ramming it and sending Margaret flying across the room. He began chasing her around the table and, because she was so traumatised, she found herself unable to scream, or call out in any way; her throat was constricted with terror. The man suddenly gave up the chase and, in an unfamiliar accent, whispered, "Now my pretty one, stay still, for I must have you." With that, he jumped on to the table with startling agility and leapt on top of the girl.

She fell to the floor by the fire and he started to molest her. He tore at her nightgown and violently kissed and bit at her neck and breasts. She felt utterly powerless and had almost resigned herself to her fate, when she spotted the hot poker in the grate. She grabbed it with her left hand and lashed it into the attacker's face. Her retaliation only served to enrage him further and he began to claw wildly at her face, but she still had hold of the poker and started clubbing him on the head with it. Having gained the advantage, she suddenly regained control of her vocal chords and screamed out, which sent her weird attacker fleeing from the room.

Margaret wasted no time in getting to her feet and could hear his footsteps running down the cellar steps. She ran into the street, half dressed and beside herself with anger, fear and humiliation. Victoria and William were just rounding the corner and came running to her aid. Several neighbours also came out to see what all the commotion was about. Margaret shrieked that the assailant had run down into the cellar but when William went down to look, he found it empty.

Although William and Victoria could see that Margaret was in a terrible state, they thought the tale of the eighteenth century attacker was a bit far-fetched and virtually accused her of having imagined him. However, this did not account for the love-bites on Margaret's neck and chest and the scratch-marks on her face. She guessed that she had been canoodling with some local boy who had fled when he heard her older sister coming home.

Margaret stuck steadfastly by her story and several weeks later, Victoria and William had to admit that they had been wrong to distrust her, when they also saw the out-dated character in the powdered wig peering out of the parlour window one Sunday morning, as they were returning from church. The Webster girls learnt from their neighbours that the previous owners had left in a hurry, claiming that the house was haunted. They said that in the middle of the night, the sinister apparition of an old-fashioned-looking man had often appeared in their daughter's bedroom, with a lecherous look in his eye.

In the winter of 1922, a water pipe burst in the Webster sisters' house and workmen were called in. While they were digging to get to the pipe, which ran under the cellar, they unearthed an unmarked red mahogany coffin. When this coffin was opened by the authorities, it revealed the skeleton of a man wearing a long white curly wig and tattered early eighteenth century clothes – exactly matching those worn by the sinister intruder who had recently attacked the younger Webster sister.

Local historians later deduced that the skeleton was that of Richard Tilly, a wealthy but notorious eighteenth century rake and Satan worshipper. Tilly was charged with sorcery, sacrilege, blackmail, rape and even a ritual murder but had bribed the magistrate and escaped sentencing by promising to live out the rest of his days in obscurity. It is thought that the satanist was secretly buried on the site of the Webster sisters' house sometime around 1730.

Inside Tilly's coffin there was found a large crumbling book entitled *Lucifer's Bible* and, on the front page, there was the sign of an upside down pentagram, the symbol of a Satanist. The text was too mildewed and faded to make any sense of, but probably contained references to satanism and black magic practices.

Understandably, even with the coffin removed, the house

was now irrevocably tainted for the Webster sisters, and Margaret, in particular, refused to spend so much as another night there. So they sold up and moved out to North Wales. Tilly's coffin was not allowed to be buried in a Christian churchyard and is thought to have been re-interred somewhere close to Bidston Hill.

THERE'S A WAR ON!

Emma Black, a listener to one of my radio programmes, sent me a fascinating cutting from a 1970s magazine, concerning a timeslip which apparently allowed a telephone conversation to take place between two people spaced thirty years apart. The following summary of this incredible exchange may seem like an episode of *The Twilight Zone*, but I have heard of three other similar cases.

One evening, an elderly woman, Alma Bristow of Bidston, tried to ring her sister who had recently lost her husband and who lived in Frodsham, in Cheshire. Alma always had difficulty dialling numbers on the old British Telecom analogue telephone, because she suffered from stabbing arthritis in her fingers. So when a man's voice answered, "Captain Hamilton here," Alma thought she had evidently mis-dialled her sister's number. Nevertheless, she politely asked if her sister was there, just in case it was the right number and a guest had answered the phone. Hamilton cut her short, "This is not a civilian number," he replied haughtily. "Who are you?"

Alma gave her name and, as she did so, she heard a sound at the other end of the telephone that she had not heard since she was a young woman – that of an air-raid siren going off.

"Blimey! Sounds like World War Two over there," she joked.

There was an uncomfortable pause, then Captain Hamilton replied, "What are you talking about, woman?"

"The air-raid siren ... sounds like the war's still on," said Alma, about to hang up.

"Of course the war's still on. Where did you get my number from?" asked Hamilton, growing steadily more exasperated.

"But the war ended years ago, in nineteen forty-five," said Alma, beginning to suspect that she was a victim of the *Candid Camera* show or something.

Captain Hamilton could be heard whispering to an associate, before resuming the surreal conversation. "What planet are you living on? It isn't nineteen forty-five yet and if we trace you, you'll be thrown into prison for this lark, you know. You're wasting valuable time, woman."

"Pardon? It's nineteen seventy-four. The war's been over for years," Alma retorted. Then she heard the unmistakable rumble of bombs being dropped coming over the telephone.

"We'll deal with you later, make no mistake about that!" snapped Captain Hamilton, slamming down the phone.

Alma waited eagerly for him to pick up the handset of his telephone once again, but he didn't, so she never found out if she had been the victim of an elaborate hoax, or whether she really had talked with someone from wartime Britain, which, of course, would suggest that the events of the past are still going on somewhere along the fourth dimension.

Is it not ironic how the clock rules all our lives, yet we still know virtually nothing about time itself? Our ignorance regarding the nature of time reminds me of a thought-provoking remark which Einstein once made: "What does a fish know about the water in which he swims all his life?"

The Sad Tale
of a Dog Named Sam

This is a well-documented story taken from the *Times* which was published in the 1860s. It is not exactly a supernatural tale, but it does illustrate the uncanny talents which animals have for navigating over immense distances.

In 1864, Joseph Myers, a young vagrant, saw an old man throw a small sack off a bridge in London. As soon as the sack hit the murky waters of the Thames, the man smiled and then hurriedly walked away. Myers noticed, with alarm, that something was moving in the sack and fearing that it might be a child, he dived into the river from the embankment and foolishly battled the strong currents as he swam out towards the struggling bundle.

When he opened the bundle, a small mongrel dog struggled free, yelping in terror. Myers grabbed the bedraggled creature by the nape of its neck and somehow managed to swim with it to safety. He decided to call the dog Thames, but since it refused to respond to that name, he went through a succession of others, until he noticed that the animal's ears flew up when he used the name Sam. So Sam it was. That young dog proved to be the most loyal companion that Joe Myers had ever had in his life and he always saw to it that he was well fed and cared for.

In the severe winter of 1866, Myers was really down on his luck and decided to travel to Birkenhead to trace a fairly wealthy relative, in the hope that he would offer him some kind of job. He stowed away on a freight train from London with Sam tucked inside his coat. The train was bound for Liverpool, but when it pulled into Harrow, just a few miles down the line, two railway guards spotted Joe

Myers and his dog and proceeded to beat him up. Sam attacked one of the guards in an attempt to defend his master but was subjected to a frenzied attack in return. As he collapsed in pain, the guard grabbed the poor thing by his tail and flung him out of the carriage. Sam landed in a snow-covered ditch and appeared to be dead, as he showed no sign of movement.

Joe Myers' injuries were so severe, that the elderly guard panicked and calculated that he would end up being found guilty of murder if the tramp died. He told Myers that he would let him stay on the train to Liverpool, as long as he kept well-hidden and said nothing to the police. Myers started to cry about his dog but the guards just ignored him and closed the doors of the carriage and the train continued on its journey.

When Myers finally reached Liverpool, he was in a dreadful physical and emotional state. Fortunately, a man who worked at the local sailors' home took pity on him, until he was fit to travel over to Birkenhead. However, when Myers finally traced his relative, he would have nothing to do with him and he ended up drifting around Birkenhead in a blizzard, fully expecting to die from hypothermia.

He was huddled up in a doorway, famished and shivering with cold, when Sam suddenly appeared before him, with his tail wagging furiously. He whined with delight when he saw his master and began licking his face. How he had managed to travel over two hundred miles to find him, was beyond comprehension. His paws were sore and bleeding and Myers could clearly feel and see his ribcage. Presently, the dog ran off and came back later with a bone, which he started to gnaw at voraciously.

Suddenly, it stopped chewing and looked at the tramp with an unnatural sympathy. He then actually dropped the bone in his Myers' lap, as if he knew that his master was starving.

"No, Sam, you eat that," Myers protested.

The poor thing seemed very feeble and, minutes later, the last dregs of his strength deserted him and he lay across Myers' arms and died as he licked his frost-bitten hand. Myers started to cry like a baby at the loss of his beloved pet – the only living creature on earth who cared whether he lived or died – and tried in vain to resuscitate the animal. A young woman, battling through the freezing winds, was so touched by the sight of the young down and out and his unfortunate dog, that she invited Joe Myers to her home, where her father and brothers fed and looked after him and nursed him back to health. He was later employed by the family and eventually ended up going into business himself. The first thing he did, when he had enough money, was to lay his faithful dog Sam to rest in a grave near Port Sunlight.

In 1866, the Mersey froze over at one point, and several people actually walked over it, so maybe that is one possible explanation of how Sam crossed the river that winter.

THE LAUGHING LADY

In October 2000, Colin and Shirley, a couple in their late sixties, moved into a house in the Devonshire Park area of Wirral. Their new neighbours seemed to be an unusually quiet bunch, and Shirley had a sneaking suspicion that their silence had something to do with the reputation of the house they had just moved into. Colin, a pragmatic, down-to-earth sort of fellow, thought the neighbours were simply rather snobby and stand-offish, but Shirley, who had maintained that she was partly psychic for years, became increasingly convinced that the old Edwardian dwelling, which they intended to make into their home, had an unpleasant supernatural aura about it.

Appropriately, it was on the night of Halloween that Shirley and Colin had their first skirmish with the ghostly goings on of the house. They were sitting in the living room, watching a soap opera on the television, when Colin suddenly heard a noise. "What was that?" he asked, his voice betraying only mild concern.

"What' was what?" Shirley asked, and turned down the volume on the remote control. In the now silent room she also heard the distinct sound of running footsteps pattering noisily up and down the stairs of the house. Colin grabbed an old poker from the empty grate and told Shirley to stay put. He strode into the hall and gazed up the stairs into the darkness of the upstairs landing. The thumping footfalls on the carpeted staircase grew considerably louder, until it sounded as if someone was heading straight towards him. He braced himself and held the poker with both hands, expecting an intruder to show himself at any moment.

Then, to his amazement, a woman in black suddenly appeared at the stop of the stairs. Not a woman of today, but obviously someone from another century, for the clothes she wore looked old and dowdy, probably Victorian. Her puffed-sleeved blouse was as black as ebony with a dull sheen, and the bell-shaped, ankle-length dress was equally dreary, such as a widow in mourning might have worn in those days. The strange female had a ghastly, ashen face with large, black, unblinking eyes. Her mouth was curled into an enigmatic smile. As Colin was nervously mouthing the question, "Who are you?" the woman vanished. According to Colin, she literally "just went", and as she did so, he distinctly felt a cool breeze brush against his cheek.

He stood still for a moment, trying to gather his thoughts and digest what he had just witnessed, then slowly turned round to see Shirley framed in the living room doorway with her hand to her mouth. Her blue eyes were transfixed to the spot where the phantom had stood before dematerialising. She had obviously seen it too ...

The couple were extremely troubled by the appearance of their unwelcome guest and decided to consult a medium. Unfortunately, he was one of the many unscrupulous fakes who prey on the gullible, including the desperate people who have discovered that their homes have unwanted spiritual inhabitants. Immediately on reaching the house, the so-called medium claimed that he detected the spirit of a woman who had died in the house in the 1950s. This apparition, he confidently asserted, had been flushed out of "a sort of suspended animation period in Limbo" because Colin had recently rewired the house. He explained that the electrical activity had caused the apparition to be "powered up", so to speak.

The medium charged the couple an extortionate sum of money, and then set about discharging the resurrected spirit with what he called "white cleansing candles", which were placed at various points around the house. Of course, this clap-trap was completely ineffective, as Shirley found out to her cost a week later.

Colin had gone out for the night and Shirley's friend from Liverpool had promised to stay with her for a few hours, but had not turned up for some reason. Shirley tried to stay calm, but in the middle of the evening, after she had conjured up enough guts to broach the sinister staircase in order to turn on a heater in the bedroom, the lights suddenly dimmed as she reached the first floor landing.

What happened next completely overwhelmed her. The

outdated woman quite literally came flying towards her down the stairs, with her arms outstretched and her feet pointing upwards at a forty-five-degree angle. She was screeching with wild demented laughter, as she shot straight towards Shirley. At the very last second she twisted away, and then flew past her down the next flight of stairs. Shirley dropped to her knees, feeling sharp, stabbing pains in her chest and scarcely able to breathe. The hysterical laughter abruptly ceased, as the lights on the stairs simultaneously returned to their normal level of brightness.

At around 11.45pm, Colin returned from his night out playing snooker with his friends to find all the lights on in the house and Shirley trembling under the duvet in the foetal position with her hands over her head. She related the spine-chilling experience she had endured earlier, and Colin took her downstairs for a coffee. He had given up cigarettes as a Millennium resolution in December 1999, but now had an uncontrollable urge to light up. Earlier that night, when he had told his friends about their resident ghost, they had just laughed, so he didn't know who to turn to and he and Shirley seriously considered moving out of the accursed house. That was just before he telephoned me at Radio Merseyside after hearing me on the *Billy Butler Show*. On hearing the traumatic story, I told him I would come out to have a look at the house and hopefully uncover something about the ghostly occupant by leafing through the old electoral registers.

The day before I arrived, another nasty occurrence took place at that dreaded house in Devonshire Park. At around midnight, Colin and Shirley were dozing off on their sofa, as they watched a late-night film on the television, when a sudden sound, coming from the hallway, woke Shirley up. It sounded like the brass letterbox flap repeatedly opening and snapping shut. Shirley prodded Colin and alerted him to the persistent noise. He grabbed a heavy ornamental candlestick from a display cabinet and crept across the living room towards the door. The only light in the room came from a small, ruby-coloured lampshade in the corner. Colin was about to switch on the main light, but then decided against it, reasoning that if someone was attempting to break into the house, the less they saw of him the better.

He gently eased the door open a few degrees and peeped into the hallway to see a long pole protruding from the open letterbox. It had a metal hook on the end and its shaft was embedded with razor blades, set at crazy angles. Colin realised that a criminal was outside the door attempting to snatch his car keys, which were lying on a table in the hallway. He knew that if he attempted to seize the pole, the razor blades would slice through his hands as the crook outside retracted it.

Shirley crept up behind him and asked, in a whisper, what was going on, but she was pushed back into the living room. Colin leant back and grabbed his mobile phone from the coffee table and started to dial 999, when he heard a voice yell out. The screams came from his doorstep and a loud rattling sound echoed through the hallway. He ran to the bay window and pulled aside the curtain. Standing on the doorstep was a shaven-headed youth. He was staring in horror at the palms of his hands, which were in shreds and dripping with blood. The end of the device he had been holding was now being violently thrust backwards and forwards through the letterbox.

Colin immediately tried to fathom out who could possibly be shoving and pulling the deadly pole from inside his hallway. As he watched, the youth stumbled away with blood pouring copiously from his hands, clearly in a state of complete shock. The pole then shot back into the house through the letterbox and landed with a clatter in the hallway. The youth shot a single puzzled glance back at Colin through the window, before running off with his crimson hands thrust under his armpits. Colin was only snapped out of his confusion when he heard a tinny-sounding voice coming from his telephone, asking which emergency service he required.

When the police arrived, they took one look at the pole with the hook and razor blades lying in the hallway and shook their heads. They had seen such lethal looking poles before and knew that their purpose was to obtain keys, or any other valuables left within reach in their victims' hallways. This pole was heavily bloodstained, but Colin was at a loss to explain who had been able to pull the pole out of the criminal's hands. That same person had possessed the strength to ram the bladed pole back at the would be thief badly lacerating his hands.

Shirley had her own theory. She believed it had all been down to their resident ghost. After all, who else could it have been? It wasn't as if the youth had had an accomplice who had turned on him. The young scally had almost definitely been alone.

When I looked into the case, I found that the house did have strange cold spots within its walls. To investigate further, I left a tape recorder with various special microphones fitted to it. One microphone was a transducer that can pick up sounds in the ultrasonic range, and it was this that detected a faint laughing sound inside the house. There was also a curious message spoken by a young female voice which clearly stated the words, "Rosalind isn't mad!"

On the following day I scoured through the electoral

registers and discovered that a woman named Rosalind Lundy had once lived at the haunted house. Alas, as I was continuing my research into the elusive Rosalind, Colin and Shirley's nerves reached breaking point. They could not endure any further middle-of-the-night visitations from the laughing lady, and they moved away to St Michael's Hamlet, in Liverpool.

At the time of writing, the house in Devonshire Park lies empty, except, of course, for the troubled vestige of that woman from long ago.

THE WITCHES OF WILLASTON

A friend of the girl featured in the following story imparted the details of this tale to me during a book signing at Waterstones in Birkenhead, a few years ago. It is also backed up by the many reports of witches seen around Willaston, Eastham and Raby Mere that I have collected over the last twelve years.

So let us set the scene – Wirral, at the witching hour of one o'clock in the morning; two infatuated fourteen-year-olds – Lynsey from Ellesmere Port and Martin from Raby – were walking along Mill Lane, Willaston, holding hands under a full moon in the August of 1972. Earlier they had been to Rivacre Baths, and then on to the birthday party of Lynsey's cousin at nearby Hillside Drive. Lynsey should have been home two hours ago, but had telephoned her mum to say that she would be staying over at a friend's house in Hooton. All a white lie, of course, because that night, Lynsey intended to stay over at her boyfriend's house. Martin's older brother Ged was holding the fort until his parents returned from a short vacation in Bognor Regis, and the plan was simple: Ged usually went to bed at around two in the morning, and when he did, Martin would smuggle Lynsey into his bedroom.

"Say he stays up all night, Marty?" Lynsey asked nervously.

"Then we'll just stay out all night and sleep under the stars," replied her boyfriend of a whole two months.

As the couple strolled along Mill Lane, they both heard what sounded like a fight, somewhere in the distance.

"Did you hear that?" asked Lynsey, standing stock still. Her eyes swivelled right and left, as she resisted an awkward kiss from Marty.

"Yeah," said Marty, unconcerned, and curled his arm around her right shoulder. But the aggressive noises had frightened her and she shoved him away, annoyed that she was not being taken seriously.

Just then screeches of laughter echoed across the fields, which were painted silver by the moon. Eerie, other worldly laughter; not the mirthful sounds of young merrymakers, nor the jocular roar of drunks staggering home. This was hysterical, sinister, frenzied laughter; and it chilled Lynsey so much, that she hugged Martin and suggested turning around.

"Don't be soft, we're nearly there," Martin assured her.

"But I've got a really nasty feeling something's out there tonight."

"What do you mean, 'something's out there'?" he scoffed, pulling her along.

Taking reluctant steps to keep up with him, she replied, "I don't know; I just feel there's something ... I don't know ... something evil ... in the air tonight."

Lynsey had begun to regret ever having agreed to Martin's plan and wished that she was safely back at home with her mother and brothers in Hampton Gardens. She had been told she was psychic by her mother on many occasions. Once she had dreamt that her father was injured in hospital, and days later, he broke both his legs when he fell off some scaffolding on a building site. Another time, she awoke at four in the morning to find her grandmother standing at the foot of her bed, waving and smiling. That same morning, at the same time, Lynsey's grandmother passed away at her home in Runcorn. Just before she died, she called out for Lynsey and was seen to smile and wave at someone who was invisible to Lynsey's aunt and the family doctor who were standing at her bedside.

And so, on this moonlit night, in that secluded lane in Willaston, Lynsey's extra-sensory powers once more had come into play. She felt a grim and powerful sense of foreboding, a conviction that she was about to meet something uncanny, horrible – and she was right!

As she and Marty passed by the sail-less remains of Willaston Windmill, they spotted two slender figures perched on the pinnacle of the conical tower, striking one another with long poles of some sort and screaming abuse.

"Who the hell are they, and what are they doing?" Marty asked, as he craned his neck to watch the suicidal combatants. If one of them were to fall off, surely that would be the end of them? What was even more mystifying was that they looked and sounded like women.

"They're witches," said Lynsey in a low voice, as if talking to herself.

"What a stupid place for a fight! They must be barmy," said Marty. "It'd serve them right if they fell off and broke their necks."

No sooner had he said this, than the two silhouetted women toppled off the old mill, but they didn't plummet to the ground as expected. Instead they floated off sideways, and as they did so, they began striking one another anew with their weapons – now clearly identifiable as brooms.

All Marty's teenage bravado evaporated, as his brain struggled to rationalise the evidence of his eyes.

"I told you they were witches," said Lynsey, rather petulantly, but she too was overawed by the spooky spectacle and was shivering with fear.

Not doubting her for a minute, Marty turned on his heels and careered back down Mill Lane, with Lynsey following close behind. He stopped several times to look back, but Lynsey urged him not to, and began to cry. This turned out to be unwise, because her loud sobs alerted the levitating women to their presence. For a few seconds they stopped, stock-still in the sky, then flew like the wind towards the fleeing couple. Marty was running off ahead of Lynsey, despite her frantic screams for him to come back and wait for her. He stole a glance over his shoulder just once, and saw the witches swooping down on his helpless girlfriend.

The boy ran to a house on Briardale Road, which was just off the dark lane and hammered on the door until an old woman answered. When he told her about the fearsome witches, her eyes widened, and she began to cackle with laughter. Now Marty was stumbling backwards down the path and on to the road, as the sprightly old woman chased after him in her long white nightdress.

Just after the creepy old crone had finally given up her pursuit, Marty spotted a policeman by Ash Tree Farm and ran to tell him about the witches' attack on his girlfriend. Far from greeting his far-fetched tale with scepticism, the constable showed grave concern and accompanied Marty to the elbow of Mill Lane, where they found Lynsey lying unconscious. They lifted her up to a sitting position and she slowly started to come round. She couldn't talk for a while, but when she did regain the power of speech, she said that the two witches – one old and one young – had dragged her into the air by her hair and attempted to drop her down into a clay pit, but she had clung on with all her might to their arms and legs. In the end, the witches had tired of tormenting her and had put her down on Mill Lane, before flying off screaming with laughter towards the north. It was at this point that poor Lynsey had passed out.

The policeman seemed to know something about the witches, although he was not prepared to divulge anything to the two youngsters. He did, however, warn them to keep well away from the area around the old windmill in the future. Their experiences that night had chilled them to the marrow and so no such warning was necessary. In fact, neither of them would venture near Mill Lane, even in broad daylight, ever again.

In 1969, there were reports of female voices and laughter in the sky over the Windle Hill area. Several children and a schoolteacher heard the unearthly sounds which apparently were coming from somewhere high above a dismantled railway track. Were the airborne sounds really the laughter and chatter of the Willaston witches?

THE SINGING SPECTRE
OF CLEVELAND STREET

In the 1960s, there was a Birkenhead pub that stood at Number 16 Chester Street called the Queen's Arms Hotel. The pub would later be renamed the Worsley Arms, and it still stands today, although whether the atmosphere there is better or worse nowadays, is open to debate.

On the Saturday evening of 30 October 1965, Tony and Margaret Kirkpatrick, of Argyle Street, had decided to go out and meet their friends at the Queen's Arms. They were both in there fifties and their two children had left home some years ago. Before going out on this chilly autumn evening, Tony had settled down to watch the popular television series *Dixon of Dock Green*, which was set in the East End of London and starred Jack Warner. Although the programme was produced by the BBC's Light Entertainment Department, the show had its moments of high drama and consistently attracted high viewing figures. Upon this October evening, Margaret had to almost wrench Tony out of his fireside armchair, because he was so wrapped up in Constable George Dixon's investigative exploits. He waited until the show had ended at 7.25pm and the last of the credits had gone up, before he could finally be persuaded to move out of the house.

He was soon walking down Argyle Street, hand in hand with Margaret and looking forward to a pleasant evening. Once inside the pub, he enjoyed the usual banter about sport and politics and then entertained his friends with amusing anecdotes from his twenty-five years as a plumber, whilst Margaret chatted to her women friends. At around 10.50pm, the two of them left the Queen's Arms, and as they were passing the premises of Greenline Taxis, they bumped into Lizzy and Frank Thackeray, a couple who used to live near them a few years back. Frank invited Tony and Margaret to an all-night party at a relative's house on Cleveland Street and, feeling in a sociable mood, they accepted. They left this party at around three in the morning, and set off to walk home. Halfway back, Tony stopped to shield his match flame as he lit up a Woodbine cigarette. Margaret, walking a few yards ahead, urged him to hurry up, as she was cold and tired and couldn't wait to get home to bed.

It was at this point that Margaret noticed a person she did not recognise emerging from the Wirral Hotel public house at Number 97 Cleveland Street; a white-haired man in a black suit, who could barely stand up and seemed incapable of walking in a straight line. Tony didn't like the look of him and instinctively took hold of Margaret's hand. They carried on with the intoxicated stranger walking about two hundred yards ahead of them.

A thin October sea-mist had blown in from the river, and the Kirkpatricks longed for the warmth of their cosy little terraced home on Argyle Street, just five minutes' walk away now. Margaret kept her eyes firmly fixed on the swaying black figure further down Cleveland Street, just in case he became aggressive, although he seemed to be very mellow and was singing an old song she hadn't heard for years – 'Don't Get Around Much Any More' – an old hit for the Inkspots, from the 1940s. She was relieved to find that the man was not a rowdy-sounding drunk, but possessed a fine, butter-smooth voice, and she found the song incredibly sad and nostalgic. The song is about someone who avoids the places he went to when he was with his partner, because they bring back painful memories.

Suddenly, the white-haired singer looked around, and slowed for a moment. He had obviously noticed them, and slunk off into a doorway. The Kirkpatricks assumed the house was the man's home, but when they passed the doorway shortly afterwards, they saw that it was boarded up. Tony was more intrigued than afraid, but Margaret sensed that there had been something not quite right about the singer in the wee small hours. Tony checked the board and the nails that fixed it to the door frame, expecting to find a loose piece of wood, but it was all perfectly intact. There was no way into the building, so where had the drunken man disappeared to?

"Come on, Tony, let's go," urged Margaret. "I don't like it one bit. I knew there was something creepy about that old man, the minute I set eyes on him."

Then, glancing up through the wispy mists at the grimy upper windows of the vacant house, she jumped when she saw a face peering down at her. For a brief second or so, she could clearly make out that the man behind the dirty glass had white hair. It had to be him, yet how could he possibly have managed to pass straight through the boarded up door? There was no obvious answer to that question and so she turned away in consternation and dragged her husband away from the derelict house.

Margaret and Tony discussed the mysterious incident at some length between themselves, but never mentioned the ghost – for that was what they were sure it was – to anyone else. So when, a few years later, their neighbour, Mrs Baxter, mentioned a ghost that was being seen in the neighbourhood, Margaret's ears instantly pricked up. Mrs Baxter described the apparition as a man in black with white hair, who seemed to come out of the Wirral Hotel pub long after the premises had closed for the night. If the ghost noticed anyone, as he swayed to and fro along the road, he would dart through walls and wait inside the nearest building until the living had passed by. According to Mrs Baxter, sightings of the singing ghost always started up again round about Halloween. Margaret went cold when she learned this, because she recalled that it had been around 3am, on 31 October, when she and her husband had had their encounter with the singing spectre.

Similar sightings of the ghost have continued for many years, always happening around October time, but no one knows whose ghost it is that is haunting Cleveland Street. People who have managed to observe the snowy-haired phantom at close quarters have noted that he looks as solid as any living person. So if you live in the Cleveland Street area watch out! You just might bump into this unidentified carnate entity the next time you pass by the Wirral Hotel pub after night has fallen.

CHILLING CHIMES

In February 2002, Barbara from Birkenhead set off with her boyfriend Liam for a car boot sale in Chester. They arrived at the sale so early, that it was still dark when they pulled into the carpark, and Liam had to fetch his flashlight from the car, in order to see what was on offer. Barbara knew from past experience that all the best items were snatched up even before their owners had had a chance to display them on their stalls.

She loved the thrill of looking for bargains, always hoping to become one of those people she had seen on 'The Antiques Road Show', who had bought something for a few pence, later to find that it was worth thousands. Within a short space of time she had found and bought a few bits and bobs, but nothing very exciting. Then one item took her fancy. It was a small, black, shiny musical box, with an intricate gold heart pattern inlaid on the lid. She had been attracted by the delicate detail on it, and was satisfied with herself for having spotted it, and for only three pounds. As soon as she had it in her possession, she opened it, and it began to play the main theme tune from the opera, 'The Merry Widow'.

When the couple arrived back home later that day, Liam suddenly called for her attention. "What's that noise?" he asked, looking around.

"What's what noise?" Barbara replied, without paying much heed – until she heard it too.

It was clearly the chimes of 'The Merry Widow', but she could not understand why they could hear the tune, as the unusual little box was not in the room, but upstairs in the bedroom. She went upstairs to check and found the closed box lying silently on her dressing table, where she had put it minutes earlier. As soon as she opened it, she heard the chimes begin, then she snapped closed the lid, silencing the music, and placed it back on the dresser.

When Barbara went to work on the following day, she could not get the haunting melody out of her mind, and neither could her boyfriend. Liam worked in a garage, and he first became aware of the spectral melody as his boss was talking to him about the day's jobs in his office. The tinny tinkling of the chimes in his head became such a distraction, that he couldn't concentrate on his work. All he could hear was the accursed tune being played over and over again in his head. Eventually, he became so beside himself, that he had to make an excuse and leave work. As he was driving home, he felt so peculiar, that he seriously wondered if someone in the garage had spiked his tea with an hallucinogenic drug.

When he got home, he was surprised to find Barbara already there. She too had come home from work driven to distraction by the haunting chimes relentlessly replaying inside her head.

Later that day, she showed her neighbour the musical box, and she immediately commented on how the music was strangely catchy; so catchy, in fact, that that evening the neighbour called round to say that the eerie tune had invaded her mind as well. It was even affecting her sleep, because she had fallen asleep on the settee and could still hear the irritating notes playing over and over again in her dreams.

A call was made to me at the studios of Radio Merseyside, and I visited Barbara and Liam's home in Birkenhead to take a look at the mysterious musical box. Wary of its reputation, I was not too keen to open it, even though my curiosity urged me to do so. Barbara, Liam and their neighbour nervously suggested that I should open the box out of their earshot.

As I examined it, I could find no markings on the outside which might have provided the name of its manufacturer. Undaunted, I later visited the car boot sale where Barbara had purchased the box, and even managed to trace the man who had sold it to her, but all he could remember was that an old woman had given him the box for nothing at another car boot sale in Rock Ferry.

I decided to mention the musical box on the radio, and described the tune it played. Immediately, a number of listeners called in to the station. Some claimed that they, too, had been afflicted with the never-ending tune after listening to the box. One woman who had visited a hearing specialist was diagnosed with tinnitus, but believed her condition had something to do with the mysterious black musical box and its ceaseless irritating melody.

Then came the breakthrough.

A caller named Mr Lewis telephoned me and was able to accurately describe the intricate heart-shaped pattern on the lid. He said that, after he had opened that exact same box in 1975, he too had been unable to get the tune out of his head. It had become so bad, that he had been forced to sleep with the radio playing on his bedside table, in order to drown out the tune.

By 1977, the tune had finally faded away out of his head, but it had caused such an unwelcome intrusion into his life, that it had broken up his marriage. I asked him how it had first come into his possession, and he said that he had moved into a house in Rock Ferry, in 1974, and had found it there, along with some other items, including an old Welsh Bible. Mr Lewis had subsequently heard a strange tale from his then new neighbours. They told him that the previous inhabitant of the house had poisoned himself many years before, in the 1920s. Beside his body, the man's wife had found the musical box lying open with the haunting melody still playing.

This is one story with no satisfactory ending. In this era, when radio stations and television programmes repeatedly bombard us with mindless pop tunes, it is easy to find ourselves humming or whistling a catchy melody, but how did an old musical box manage to implant such a devilishly interminable tune into the minds of those who innocently opened its lid? And what is the significance of 'The Merry Widow?'

I remain baffled.

THE VARDØGER

I have written about the phenomenon of doppelgangers many times before. They are the sinister doubles of living people, and are often mistaken for them. When they are seen in the vicinity of the person whom they strongly resemble, onlookers usually assume that they are looking at twins, because the doppelganger is literally a flesh-and-blood replica, who may even be wearing the exact same clothes as his or her real counterpart.

An associated phenomenon of the doppelganger is the vardøger – a Norwegian word that translates as 'forerunner'. In the Occult sphere, vardøger is a term meaning 'a premonitory sound or sight of a person before he or she arrives.' The following case is an instance of the vardøger phenomenon in action, and it took place in Wirral.

The rectangular Wirral peninsula is only about ten miles long and seven miles wide, yet holds many a hidden secret within its leafy lanes and pretty villages. Many Wirralians have travelled the country, and indeed the world, unaware of the beautiful and fascinating places that exist on their own doorstep.

During the long-gone summer of 1970, two young women from Birkenhead, Terri Inskip and Ruth Wescombe, along with the latter's seventeen-year-old cousin Simon Wescombe (from Wallasey), decided to take a train-ride to Port Sunlight. Terri and Ruth – who were both nineteen at the time – had set out on a mission to try and track down a boy who had gone to the same secondary school as themselves, as Terri still had a strong crush on him. The boy's name was Paul Peake.

Upon arriving at Port Sunlight, the trio were impressed

by the chocolate box prettiness of the garden village, and after buying sweets at a corner shop, they visited the Lady Lever Art Gallery, and it was here that something rather peculiar took place.

As Terri entered the building's grand foyer, a smartly-dressed elderly man nodded to her and smiled in a friendly way. Terri smiled back out of courtesy, although she had no idea who he was, and then trailed after the others to the start of the exhibition. As she wandered along from painting to painting, the same man tapped her on the shoulder and said, "I never knew you were an art lover".

Ruth and Simon, nudged each other and smirked, because it was obvious from the confused expression on Terri's face that she hadn't got a clue as to the man's identity, but again, simply out of good manners, she smiled at him, then moved quickly along to join her sniggering friends. When she was still within earshot, the old man called after her, "Terri ... where's Paul? You haven't had a row, have you?"

His words had an electrifying effect and Terri froze. Ruth shot her a quizzical look. Terri whipped round and looked directly at the old grey-haired man. "Pardon?" she said, mindful of the fact that she had had Paul Peake on the brain for weeks, and here was a complete stranger mentioning someone called Paul as if her were her long-term boyfriend.

"Sorry to pry, dear," he said. "It's just that I've never seen you out and about without him before."

"Without Paul?' Terri replied, taken aback.

"Yes ... I do apologise, for poking my nose in," said the old man, rather sheepishly, and then shuffled out of the gallery without further explanation.

On three further occasions that day, Terri was greeted by someone who appeared to know her well, yet she had no idea who any of them were. In the first instance, a man of around thirty, with a slight Irish accent, was walking down Bolton Road, when he stopped and enquired about her mother's health, as he had heard that she had recently gone into hospital. Terri's mother was in the best of health, and she curtly told the man that she didn't know him and had no idea what he was talking about. The man appeared perplexed, "You're Terri, Terri Inskip, aren't you?" he replied. Then he half-turned his head and gave her a wry smile, as though she was pulling his leg by pretending not to know him. When Terri insisted that she had never set eyes on him before, he shook his head in irritation and walked off into one of the cottages on the road.

By this time, Terri was feeling pretty irritated herself and more than a little unnerved by the two cases of mistaken identity.

"Let's go home," suggested Simon. He had had enough of the spooky encounters, but he was overruled by the girls, whose natural curiosity had got the better of them. A little later they were strolling aimlessly down Corniche Road, when a middle-aged woman passed by, halted, and did a double-take at Terri. "I thought you'd gone to Birkenhead?" said the woman.

The incident triggered a strong feeling of déjà vu in Terri – the sensation of somehow knowing what would happen next. She couldn't think of a suitable reply and just shook her head meekly.

"Here we go again," said Simon, as an aside.

"What's wrong?" asked the woman. She seemed genuinely concerned about Terri, and was not threatening in any way.

"I think you're mistaking me for someone else," Terri told her.

"Look, I really think we should be going now," said Simon, and he and Ruth started heading for the train station on Greendale Road, with Terri running along behind. When they reached the station, a young man of about twenty was standing on the platform, smoking a cigarette. As soon as he set eyes on Terri, he sidled over and asked, with a cheeky grin on his face, if she was "the bird" who was getting married to Paul Peake.

Terri was speechless.

"What's up, love? Been struck dumb or something?" asked the cocky youth. A woodbine cigarette was protruding from the gap of an absent tooth, and as he spoke, bits of ash dropped off the end. "Did he get you preggers or something?"

Terri turned away in disgust and pretended to be reading the train timetable. Luckily, the train arrived just then, and she, Ruth and Simon climbed aboard and sat as far away from the sleazy, greasy-haired nosy parker as possible. He slouched down in a seat at the other end of the carriage, blowing smoke rings, which were obviously designed to impress Terri. At one point he got up and was just about to sit down next to her, when she told the ticket inspector that he was bothering her. The railway official had a word with the seedy-looking pest, who reluctantly slunk back to his original position, but still kept his eyes fixed on her.

The train pulled in at Bebington station, and whilst they were waiting for it to restart, Terri happened to look across the tracks to a train passing slowly on the parallel track at the other side of the station. It was moving sufficiently slowly for Terri to be able to make out the faces of all the passengers on board. She sat up with a start when she saw an exact replica of herself, sitting next to Paul Peake! She drew Ruth and Simon's attention to her double, but they couldn't see a thing. This sighting of her doppelganger turned Terri's blood to ice, and she refused to go anywhere near Port Sunlight again.

Around 1972 she heard along the grapevine that Paul Peake had broken off his engagement with the 'other Terri' – a girl the Birkenhead Terri regarded as a sinister impostor. He later went to work in the Middle East for a few years, before emigrating to Australia. In 1981, Ruth Wescombe bumped into Paul in Alice Springs, and she told him about the weird case of an apparent doppelganger, but Paul insisted that the girl he had been engaged to at that time, was, without a shadow of a doubt, Terri Inskip.

The mystery will probably never be solved, and for all we know, perhaps Terri's doppelganger is still at large in the world – and, well, for that matter, for all you know, perhaps *your* doppelganger is out there somewhere as well ...

THE GHOSTS OF BRIMSTAGE

In 1988, Jason, a man in his thirties, left his home in Reeds Road, Huyton, after becoming the victim of a sinister but short-lived poltergeist outbreak. The phenomenon began innocently enough with a very faint tapping sound on his bedroom window, which, at first, Jason believed to be caused by moths banging against the window panes, but this turned out not to be the case. The tapping sounds then moved to the wardrobe, and would come on a regular basis, which Jason found harder to explain away. He started sleeping with the DAB radio on, in an effort to drown out the eerie tappings. Three days into the spooky goings-on, something kept switching the radio to Classic FM. At the end of his tether, Jason sat up in his dark bedroom one night and addressed the nuisance spirit. First he swore, then he shouted, "Stop this, or I'll exorcise you."

He punched his pillow in anger and frustration – and not a little fear – then attempted to rest his head on it, but the pillow unaccountably kept sliding off the bed.

"That's it!" Jason shouted, with goosebumps forming on his arms, "I've just about had ..." but he could not finish, because the pillow was being pressed down on his face with tremendous force, as if at least two people were bearing down on him. He blindly thrashed out with his fists and feet, but they did not make contact with anyone. Just when he was close to losing consciousness, the pillow lifted off his face and flew across the room. Gasping for air, Jason rolled off the bed, and staggered towards the light switch. The room was filled with the overpowering smell of strong pipe tobacco, which was inexplicable, because he didn't even smoke cigarettes.

That same day, Jason packed up his belongings and left Reeds Road for good. He stayed with a friend in Walton for a few weeks, then decided to rent an apartment in Higher Bebington. Two months later, he found employment at a printworks near Heswall, and one evening, in the autumn of 1983, he had been working an overtime shift, and so did not quit the premises until 8.20pm. He drove homewards up the A5317 through a light drizzle, passing the sleepy village of Brimstage on the way. Minutes later, he swerved left into the sweeping bend of Brimstage Road, where he suddenly came across a man standing right in the middle of the road. He braked as hard as he could – causing his head to strike the windscreen, because, foolishly, he had not bothered to put on his seat-belt.

Luckily, Jason suffered only slight concussion, and soon regained his senses. He rushed out of his car and hurried towards the man, whom he guessed was aged about sixty, and who was still standing there, in the middle of the road, seemingly in a total trance. He wore a green jacket and was holding what looked like a petrol can in his left hand.

"Are you completely mad or something?" Jason asked, seething with anger. "You could have killed me and yourself, you fool!"

The grey-haired stranger didn't even acknowledge him. He just stared with a fixed gaze towards the dark fields behind Jason. When Jason was within six feet of him, the man vanished in an instant and the whole road was suddenly lit up and a rushing sound filled Jason's ears. A car screeched to a halt, narrowly missing his car, which he had left parked on the bend. The passenger of the car shouted a string of abuse at Jason, then drove off.

Jason quickly jumped back into his car and set off home, passing Brimstage Hall, a mysterious mansion that may date back to the twelfth century. The first recorded occupants of the hall were Sir Hugh Hulse and his wife Marjorie, who were granted the right to build a chapel there in 1398 – on a site which encompassed the vestiges of an even earlier structure of unknown origin. There are psychics who believe that this enigmatic hall is the focal point of a powerful force which is somehow responsible for the high number of paranormal incidents that have taken place in the immediate vicinity.

A week after the near-miss with the man in the green jacket, Jason came across him again. This time, the encounter took place earlier in the evening, at around 7.30pm, again after Jason had put in some overtime at the printworks. He passed the apparition at the place where Brimstage Road forks into Brimstage Lane. He pulled over and turned in his seat to witness the ghost walk up

Brimstage Lane into the darkness. He waited for about five minutes, wondering if he would come back into the well-lit area of Brimstage Road, then decided to drive on, because the road seemed unusually quiet – not a single car had passed him.

He turned back to face the wheel – and there was the ghost in the green jacket again, standing in front of the car, about twelve feet away. He was holding the same petrol can in his left hand, and walked slowly towards Jason, and this time he did not wear the vacant far-away expression of the week before. Instead, the ghost's face was bursting with sinister glee, and its eyeballs were white and bulging.

Jason started up the car and the headlights blazed into life, catching the solid-looking phantom in their glare. The ghost thrust out the can with its arm, as if making a request for petrol from Jason, but the latter tore off up Brimstage Road in no mood to play the good Samaritan. A glance into his rear-view mirror told him that the ghost of the road had performed his vanishing act once again. Throughout the remainder of the journey home, Jason kept dreading the reappearance of the ghost, but he did not see it again, either on that night or on any other.

Until he left Wirral to live in Chester, in 1991, Jason refused to travel down Brimstage Road on his way to and from work, even in broad daylight. It is ironic that he had left Huyton because of a terrifying experience with a poltergeist, only to meet another paranormal entity in Wirral! Of course, this may not have been a coincidence at all, but an indication that he was psychic.

Time after time I have received emails and letters from readers about the ghost of Brimstage Road, and despite exhaustive research, I still have no idea whose earthbound ghost is haunting that long and winding road. I have heard many stories and theories about the origins of the ghost, but cannot accept any of them without proof.

Some say the ghost is that of a motorist who ran out of petrol on Brimstage Road in the 1970s, and, going in search of a filling station, was knocked down by a car. Others claim that a man who discovered that his wife was having an affair, dowsed himself with petrol on the road in the 1960s and set fire to himself, but again, there are no records (as far as I can discern) of any such event. Other versions say the ghost stares towards Clatterbridge Hospital away in the distance, where his wife died many years ago, but why does he choose to stand in the middle of the road with a petrol can?

As I mentioned before, the man in the green jacket is not the only ghost who haunts the area around Brimstage Hall. On many occasions since the 1970s, a young woman of around twenty has flagged down cars on Brimstage Road, but never gets into any of the ones that stop for her – and she never speaks.

In the 1990s, a man named Roger was driving to see his wife in St John's Hospice on one pleasant summer evening, when he saw a young blonde-haired woman waving to him in a frantic fashion near Junction 4 of the M53, close to Brimstage Road. He pulled over, as she seemed to be in some distress, but as soon as he stopped, she threw her hands to her mouth and vanished.

A ghostly cyclist is seen travelling down Red Hill Road, sometimes all the way down to Brimstage Lane, but he often vanished as he passes under the M53. This ghost has been seen at very close quarters by several people, and one man, Bill Turner of Prenton, even recognised the model of bicycle the ghost was riding.

In July 2007, fifty-nine-year-old Bill was taking photographs around Storeton one morning, when he decided to walk down Brimstage Lane to take some shots of Brimstage Hall. He heard a whirring sound behind him, and a few seconds later he saw a man of about thirty, riding past on the kind of bike he hadn't set eyes on since the 1960s – a grass-green James Comet Roadster. Bill had ridden such a bike in his youth, and wondered if the cyclist would mind if he took a photograph of it. The cyclist negotiated the slight bend as Bill got his camera ready to take the shot. But he was to be disappointed, because, a moment later, he watched agape as the James Comet Roadster and its rider slowly faded away.

Bill stood looking at the spot for ages, wondering if he was losing his mind and had started imagining things. A middle-aged woman passed by and saw him standing there, and stopped to ask if he was alright. Bill found himself telling the woman what he had just seen. She nodded knowingly and said, "I've seen him myself. He comes right down from Red Hill Road and just vanishes when he gets to here." Bill was very relieved to know that someone else had seen the ghost. As with the other two ghosts of Brimstage, the identity of the ghostly cyclist has never been ascertained.

THE TRANMERE TERROR

I have studied and investigated ghosts and ghostly encounters for many years, and have established from first-hand experience that there are some apparitions that can cause physical or psychological harm. Despite the often-repeated claims that ghosts are not able to harm the living, there are many cases on record of supernatural entities that have inflicted serious injuries on those unfortunate enough to encounter them. An unsettling example of a ghost that harmed the living, was the so-called 'Tranmere Terror' – the ghastly apparition of a sinister gibbering face that terrorised people from Tranmere and Bebington and other parts of Wirral.

The first visitations began in the early 1950s, when a night-watchman was sitting at his brazier, in the dead of night, at some roadworks on Church Road, close to St Catherine's Hospital in Tranmere. The time was 3am, when the night-watchman suddenly beheld an evil-looking face leering at him out of the blackness as he sat in his little booth. There was no question that the face was some kind of supernatural presence, surrounded as it was by an aura of fiery feathery luminescence. As if that were not startling enough, the head had no body attached to it, and bobbed before him for a while with a hideous, gibbering expression. The night-watchman let out a strangled yelp and cringed with fear. Fortunately, the flame-lurid face then floated off backwards and vanished into the night, leaving the poor man trembling with shock.

Two more night-watchman in other parts of Wirral, encountered the same alarming apparition over the next fortnight, and then the Tranmere Terror, as the press soon nicknamed him, started to cast his net wider and began to haunt other members of the public. It was rumoured that one man who had beheld the terrifying face had been so terrified that he had died on the spot from heart failure.

A full-blown scare ensued, in which rumour and exaggeration created an atmosphere of unbridled panic, and the people living in Tranmere and its surrounding areas barricaded themselves into their homes after nightfall. Some believed that the Devil himself was at large in the suburbs of Birkenhead, whilst others were more sceptical and suspected that a twisted hoaxer was at work, taking a malign pleasure intimidating his innocent neighbours. But those who had received a visit from the Terror, and seen his ghastly face, were not to be fobbed off with such simple and blasé explanations. What they had seen had been no human hoaxer, of that they were certain.

One brave individual who dared to venture out into the night to track down the dreaded demon, was seventy-two-year-old Liverpudlian, George Garridon. He had held a life-long interest in all things supernatural, and was determined to witness the Tranmere Terror for himself and put an end to all the spurious rumours and speculation. He did not have long to wait!

Garridon's mission to confront the mysterious bogeyman was accomplished at a street off the Old Chester Road, where the glowing face had materialised to terrorise the staff of an old warehouse. Garridon got wind of the incident and rushed to the scene to find people scattering in all directions away from the warehouse. When he tried to talk to them, they just charged past him in blind panic.

The intrepid pensioner then entered the building and immediately came upon the Terror drifting towards him across the vast space, which was strewn with boxes that had been abandoned by the fleeing workforce in their hurry to get away. Instead of joining them, Garridon stood his ground and attempted to communicate with the apparition. The Terror responded instantly and dramatically. Orange and scarlet tongues of flame issued from its hovering head, and at the same time, in a deep and ominous voice, it spoke several words that were not recognised by Garridon. The pensioner could speak five languages, yet could make no sense of the Terror's alien and exotic tongue.

The ghost then fell silent and its glowing red eyes suddenly seemed to fill with sorrow before they finally closed, and the head vanished into thin air. Far from being left a trembling wreck by all this, Garridon was delighted that he had at last realised his lifetime's ambition, and come face to face with a genuine ghost.

The apparition was seen no more after that spectacular confrontation, and the Tranmere Terror remains yet another of Merseyside's unsolved supernatural mysteries.

THE BLACK COMB

In the 1930s, forty-five-year-old John Negus was employed as a crane operator at Storeton quarry in Bebington. The high quality stones which were hewn from the quarry on a daily basis, were not only used locally to build the magnificent villas around Birkenhead Park; so highly prized was Storeton stone that it was also exported to New York, to clad such prestigious buildings as the world famous Empire State skyscraper.

During the continuous excavations and chiselling at Storeton quarry in 1935, it is said that a strange artefact was unearthed. Embedded in the rock John Negus came upon a peculiar black comb, made of some marble-like material, which, after it had been carefully extracted, was found to have just nine teeth. Instead of handing over the apparently stone-aged comb to archaeologists, he wrapped it up in a handkerchief and took it home to his house in Rock Ferry.

After tea, he produced the handkerchief and proudly showed the comb to his wife Teresa, who reacted in a very unexpected way as soon as she set eyes on it. Without even touching the comb, she told him to throw it away at once. Teresa was psychic, and was able to detect eerie impressions of death and evil coming from the comb. John Negus had always dismissed his wife's alleged psychical skills as so much mumbo jumbo – "psychy mumbo jumbo" – he called them. He felt that they were just the result of her having been brought up by an eccentric superstitious mother and a fanatically religious father. And so he chose to ignore her advice and hid the comb between a pile of newspapers, unaware that his son was watching.

That night though, John Negus had a strange dream

about the contentious comb, in which there was a woman with long blonde hair sitting on a stool in some old dark room. The woman was leaning forward, with her hair completely covering her face, and she was combing her locks with the very comb that he had brought home from the quarry. In the dream, John was a bystander and, as he looked on, he intuitively sensed that the woman would try and kill him as soon as she stopped combing her hair. His conviction was soon proved to be true. The woman in black started to run the comb more and more slowly through her hair, until, all of a sudden, she raised the comb above her head, where it instantly metamorphosed into a long-bladed knife. At the moment when she was about to fling the knife at John, he yelled out and woke up in a cold sweat.

That same terrifying nightmare replayed itself three more times that night in the crane operator's dreaming mind. In the end, he refused to go back to sleep, because he sensed that if the woman should succeed in throwing the knife at him, he would die in his sleep from the shock.

Teresa was annoyed with him for ignoring her wishes and pleaded with him to throw away the accursed comb, and this time John readily agreed, but when he got out of bed to look for it, he couldn't find the ancient relic. He found out the next day that their nine-year-old son had been playing with the comb, having retrieved it from between the newspapers, and had now mislaid it. They searched high and low but were unable to find the haunted object.

John could not rest, not knowing the comb's whereabouts, and sat up in bed that night, trying to control his feelings of mounting dread, as sleep insidiously crept over him. He described over and over again, in great detail, how he had seen the comb turn into a knife in the woman's hand, and how she had been about to kill him. The knife had been in mid-air each time as he had awakened – just in time. Teresa listened with a grave look on her face and begged him to sleep at her mother's house that night, but John would hear none of it, and was even wondering if the dreams were a sign that he was losing touch with reality.

At three in the morning, Teresa dozed off for a while, and when she woke up again, she instinctively felt for her husband, but instead found a cold empty space beside her. She assumed that he had either taken her advice and left the house to sleep at her mother's, or had gone downstairs to sit up until morning. Then she found him – lying motionless on the floor at the side of the bed, and she became hysterical. He was lying on his back, with his eyes staring in abject terror at the ceiling, and his hands clutching at his chest. Even before she felt his pulse, she knew that he was dead.

It is said that the black comb was found not long afterwards at the Negus household, and that, since then, it has changed hands and claimed lives many more times, and is now in the Liverpool area. Over and over again I have heard accounts of the terrifying dream that features a woman combing her hair with a comb that changes into a knife. It seems that if you can wake yourself up before she stops her combing you are safe – if not, the comb changes into a knife and she throws it at your chest, impaling the heart in one expert throw – and you die in your sleep.

The Haunted Photograph Album

In 2002, Betty, a pensioner from Wallasey, telephoned me at Radio Merseyside with a strange and unsettling tale. She explained that in October 1999, she was rummaging through the stalls of a car boot sale in Birkenhead, when she came across an old, leather-bound photograph album, which contained some very old, sepia-toned pictures of people in Victorian clothes. Half of the album's yellowed pages were blank, but most of the photographs it contained featured two women and a sickly-looking little girl of about six or seven years of age. The two older women looked like a mother and daughter, and the mother's stance and expression in each shot gave the impression of stern severity. To Betty's eyes, she looked almost wicked.

Betty was intrigued by the old pictures and purchased the album for just fifty pence. That was when strange things started to happen.

One morning, Betty came into her living room and found the Victorian album lying open on the table, which was odd, because she distinctly remembered putting it away in a cupboard the night before. On the following night, Betty fell asleep, and had a terrifying dream. In the dream she was wearing iron callipers on her leg, and was trying to climb up a flight of stairs to get away from a wicked-looking old woman who was dressed in a high-collared blouse. The harsh-looking woman wore her hair up in a tight bun on the top of her head, and even in her dream, Betty recognised her at once. She was the woman featured in the dusty old photograph album. Betty was troubled and tormented in her dream, as she somehow sensed that the woman was trying to kill her. She was chasing her up the stairs, and Betty was struggling to escape her clutches, hampered as she was by the heavy and awkward callipers on her leg. The dream grew even more disturbing when the old woman seized her by the throat and started to throttle her.

The pensioner woke up in a cold sweat, aware of the rapid pounding beats of her heart as she lay in the darkness of her bedroom, her body totally paralysed. After some time, she slowly regained her composure and was able to exert sufficient willpower to cause her big toe to flex, and then slowly regained movement in the rest of her body.

She was still so bothered by the disturbing dream that she felt compelled to go downstairs and take another look at the old woman in the album. It was lying open inside the cupboard, and on the faded page was a photograph of the sinister old woman, who was smiling out at Betty. She could not for the life of her remember seeing such a picture of the long-dead woman in the album before. The very touch of the album's parchment pages now gave her the creeps and she slammed it shut and stuffed it inside a large ornamental biscuit tin.

For the next three nights, Betty had a terrible recurring nightmare, in which she was lying on a bed, unable to move. In every instance she felt as if she was the young girl in the photo album. Each time in the harrowing nightmare, she saw the shadow of the woman with the bun in her hair sliding across the wall, then her evil grinning face would loom over her. The woman would then push a pillow over her face, and she could feel the powerful pressure pushing down on her mouth and nose and eyes. Betty would fight for breath at this point, and would end up feeling as though she was suffocating. What made it more unbearable was the paralysis, the inability to move, and the haunting sound of her heart pounding away in her ears. Betty would wake up every time gasping for air, and unable to move a muscle for a several minutes.

Enough was enough. Betty was determined to find out who the people in the photo album were and what real events the haunting episodes related to. She scrutinised the book, and discovered the faint words 'Mary Meer' written on the first page. She contacted a friend who was interested in genealogy and tracing family trees, and over a six month period, he pieced together the story of the Meer family, who had lived in the area in the 1890s. What he told Betty both shocked and upset her, but did not entirely surprise her.

Mary Meer had a daughter, Philomena Meer, and a granddaughter, Francesca Meer, and it was the latter who had been paraplegic. The child had ended up as a bedridden cripple, and a rumour persisted in the Meer family for years, that Mary had killed young Francesca in her bed. The motive for the alleged murder is unknown. Perhaps it was a so-called mercy killing, because Francesca was paralysed, and maybe was not expected to live much longer. All this information led Betty to believe that the photo album was somehow haunted by the dead Victorian girl's spirit. As she had no wish to endure the paralysing nightmares ever again, she gave the book of photographs away.

THE GHOSTLY AVIATOR
OF DACRE HILL

In March 1979, Frank and Maureen, a couple in their forties from the Kirkby area of Liverpool, went to live at Dacre Hill, near Rock Ferry. Maureen worked as a shop assistant in Birkenhead and Frank held a job at a Port Sunlight factory. The couple soon settled into their three-bedroom terraced home – that is, until one rainy night in April 1979. Exhausted after a hard day's work, they both climbed into bed at midnight, and before Maureen could switch off the bedside light, Frank had fallen fast asleep. She smiled and yawned, as she reached over and was about to switch off the light – when she thought she heard voices. She shook Frank awake, and in a grumbling voice he asked what the matter was. "Listen ..." she whispered.

Frank just grunted and didn't even open his eyes, and started to drift back off into the sleep he valued so much. Maureen strained her ears and held her breath, as she listened to the slow gentle footsteps on the stairs. There was no doubt about it, someone was coming up to the bedroom and the gentle footfalls of the eerie midnight walker halted right outside the bedroom door.

Maureen stopped breathing as she watched the door knob squeak faintly as it slowly turned and then the door began to open. She found she couldn't scream, nor could she shake her husband awake. The only light coming into the room was the orange glow from a lamppost, filtering through the drawn curtains, but even by that subdued light, Maureen could make out a man, about six feet tall, creeping into the room. He wore a type of helmet with goggles, a waist-length leather jacket and dark trousers. He looked for all the world like an old-fashioned pilot. Maureen felt as if she was inside some terrifying nightmare from which she couldn't awaken.

The aviator inched closer towards her side of the bed with a smile on his sinister pale face. Maureen tried to close her eyes, but found she could no longer shut her eyelids. Then the pilot leaned over her and put his gloved hand over her mouth. His face was about five inches away from hers, and she found herself looking directly into his dark menacing eyes. Then she became aware of the distinctive drone of aeroplanes, followed by what sounded like the screeching descent of a plane in trouble. The sound got louder and louder, until it was deafeningly loud, as if the plane was about to crash into the house.

Something snapped, as if some kind of spell had been broken, and in an instant Maureen closed her eyes, pushed away the leather gloved hand, and let out an ear-piercing scream. The aviator was suddenly gone, and Frank was sitting bolt upright in bed. Maureen clung to him, shaking, and told him about the creepy man dressed as a pilot who had tried to suffocate her by pressing his hand over her mouth.

Frank, now totally alert and pumped full of adrenaline, reached under the bed and grabbed the hammer that he kept especially for burglars, and went in search of the intruder. He returned minutes later, saying that there was no sign of anyone having broken in, and he finally managed to convince Maureen that she had merely had an abnormally realistic nightmare. Nevertheless, it was not until two o'clock in the morning that she was finally able to calm down sufficiently to be able to fall asleep.

A few weeks later, Maureen returned home late from Liverpool one evening, to find Frank frantically stripping the wallpaper off their bedroom walls; Frank, who hated any form of DIY and usually had to be nagged into doing any decorating. So Maureen's first question was why on earth was he was stripping the walls at half-past-eleven at night. He wouldn't answer at first, but just carried on scraping away as if his life depended on it. However, later on, downstairs in the kitchen, he revealed the reason for his odd behaviour over a cup of tea. What he said struck a chord with Maureen and left her feeling very jittery.

Apparently, Frank had returned from the pub earlier in the evening, at about ten o'clock and whilst sitting on the bed, taking off his boots, he thought he saw a dark shape flitting across the was facing him. He had been drinking a potent wine earlier in the evening called Bentox, and a friend had also convinced him to drink a few pints of bitter on top. He therefore initially thought he might be having some kind of alcohol-induced hallucination, when more dark shapes started to flit across the wallpaper.

Deciding that the best place for someone in his state was in bed, he undressed, climbed under the covers and closed his eyes. However, he was soon startled by a deep chuckling noise, and it sounded very close by. He took a quick look around the room and reassured himself that there was no one there. The sound of people laughing must have drifted into the room from the street, he reasoned. Then Frank glanced at the section of the wall illuminated by the orange light from the street lamp. The same dark shapes were back on the wall.

He slowly got out of bed and switched on the bedside lamp. The shapes remained on the wall, and when Frank focused his bleary eyes on them, he saw the silhouettes of two biplanes engaged in a dogfight. The planes looped the loop and performed all sorts of daring aerobatics across and through the dreary old wallpaper, and during the aerial combat, Frank heard the rapid clattering sound of their machine guns. Moments later, the planes from the era of the Red Baron faded away and a tense silence pervaded the bedroom. What was going on? Frank then had the overpowering sense of being watched by someone, so he hurriedly grabbed his shirt and trousers and went downstairs.

He had overindulged in drink before with unwelcome consequences, but had never suffered any kind of hallucinations as a result. He therefore, irrationally, decided to remove the old wallpaper, which, in his befuddled state, he identified as the root cause of the trouble. After listening quietly to all this, Maureen reminded Frank about the 'nightmare' she had had, about the pilot wearing his flying goggles, and they both agreed that there was more than likely some connection.

After that night, there was no more supernatural activity at the house for over a month, until, one afternoon, Maureen's twelve-year-old nephew came to visit. He was standing in the hallway, chatting to his Aunty Maureen, when he suddenly stopped mid-sentence and stared up the stairs at something. "Who's that?" he asked.

Maureen looked up the stairs, and standing on the landing was the very pilot who had confronted her in the bedroom on that unforgettable night. He was in his full flying uniform and helmet, and was smiling down at herself and her nephew. Rendered speechless, Maureen quickly ushered her nephew over to the neighbours' house next door, where they both recovered from their ordeal over a cup of tea and a biscuit.

Maureen and Frank were both in agreement; they did not care to share their house with a pilot – no matter how friendly – or any of his aviator friends, and so they moved to a house in Lower Bebington. The identity of the ghostly aviator of Dacre Hill still remains unknown. What makes this case even more unusual is the fact that a ghostly World War One pilot, matching the description and behaviour of the Dacre Hill entity, used to terrorise a six-year-old girl at her home on Edge Lane in the Kensington area of Liverpool. The ghost used to gesture to her to be quiet by putting his finger to his lips when he appeared in her bedroom. On one occasion the begoggled pilot clamped his hand over the terrified girl's mouth, but vanished when she struggled and let out a muffled scream.

Are the ghosts of Dacre Hill and Edge Lane returned pilots from some long-disbanded spectral squadron's fatal mission? Or are the two weird aviators one and the same ghost?

DOUBLE TROUBLE

Some occultists say that we all have a ghostly twin, or doppelganger, but the twin usually keeps out of sight in normal circumstances. However, when we are ill, over-stressed, or experiencing a great crisis of some kind, our doppelganger is increasingly likely to manifest itself, and tradition states that if you see your own double, you will be dead within a year. I have been researching the phenomenon of doppelgangers long enough to know that the appearance of a flesh and blood replica of a person hardly ever spells doom, and the following little gem is a case in point.

It was the marriage that twenty-two-year-old Catherine Emily Cox had dreamt about for over five years, and on the sunny Saturday morning of 14 January 1882, the dream had finally become a reality. She stood with James Walker before the altar of St Werburgh's Church on Grange Road,

Birkenhead. The couple stole secret glances at one another until the minister gave a little cough as a signal that he was about to begin and the congregation immediately fell silent. He looked first at the couple and then at the congregation, as he started to recite the words of the wedding ceremony and was solemnly intoning the usual declaration, "If any man can show any just cause why these two people may not be joined together, let him speak now, or forever hold his peace" when all heads shot round as a man shouted, "Stop!" from the back of the church.

The voice belonged to a tall stout police constable, who came waddling down the aisle with his truncheon drawn. Women gasped in astonishment, and some wondered if the policeman was some secret jealous lover of Catherine Emily. However, PC Williams had no interest in Catherine, it was James Walker that he was after. Having reached the front of the aisle, he grabbed at the lapels of the astonished bridegroom's expensive suit and declared, "Got you! Now down to the station with you!"

"What the devil are you talking about?" protested James Walker, trying to extricate himself.

"Gawd! The gall of you! It's always the same with you jokers when you get caught isn't it? Not laughing now are you?" said the deep-voiced policeman, staring Walker straight in the eyes, with an expression just as angry as the bridegroom's own.

At this point, the best man, John Porter, stepped forward and asked the policeman what his friend was being arrested for, and the constable revealed that James Walker had knocked his helmet off in Birkenhead Park, less than quarter of an hour ago, and he had chased him all the way to St Werburgh's. Apparently, the mischievous bridegroom had even turned to pull faces at his pursuer, and had then taunted him with obscene language.

The poor bride, Catherine Emily, looked pale and unsteady on her feet, as if she was about to faint.

"But, officer, you are mistaken," argued John Porter, "because my friend has been in this church for the past half hour, and most of the people here will confirm this."

The minister, the best man, several guests and members of the Walker family, all stated that James Walker had indeed been at the church for the last half hour, waiting for his bride, who had been long overdue. Before that, Walker had been at home preparing for the ceremony, and there were several respectable witnesses who could vouch for his whereabouts.

"Then you've got a twin brother with the same red carnation in his lapel, sir," said PC Williams, flushing with embarrassment. Reluctantly he let go of the bridegroom, then turned and walked out of the church with as much dignity as he could muster under the circumstances.

John Porter looked at his friend Walker knowingly and said, "If that policeman only knew the truth of the matter!"

Porter was well aware of James Walker's troublesome doppelganger – a sinister ghostly twin that had haunted the young man since his teens. On one of the most important days of his life, Walker's double had almost ruined his wedding. The cheeky doppelganger didn't stop there and allegedly made love to James Walker's wife a year later! She had no idea what had happened until she heard footsteps coming up the stairs afterwards. She trembled and hid under the blankets, thinking it was a burglar. Instead, her husband came into the room, apologising profusely for the long delay in getting home from the office. Catherine didn't know what to make of it, as she had retired early to bed with her 'husband', and the couple had just made love. Catherine then suddenly noticed that there was no one lying next to her in the bed, and it gradually dawned on her that her husband's accursed double had masqueraded as James and taken advantage of her.

Walker had many theories about his badly-behaved carbon copy counterpart, including one that the doppelganger was actually the ghost of his twin brother who had died at the age of two. There is also a report that the doppelganger outlived the original copy, and was spotted amongst the mourners at the graveside during James Walker's funeral in the 1930s.

Mirages of Murder

On the warm Sunday night of 5 June 1887, a full moon shone down on the elegant Georgian residences of Hamilton Square, in Birkenhead. It was almost midnight, and the square was deserted except for Police Constable Reid, who had just walked into the square on his beat, his measured footsteps echoing over to the recently opened Town Hall. The beat was new and unfamiliar to PC Reid, who for the past year had patrolled the streets of Tranmere. He had been assigned to this beat just three days before. The twenty-minute foot patrol took him around the square, up Cleveland Street and down Duke Street, where he would nod to a colleague on the adjoining beat. Reid would then proceed up Conway Street, and back to Hamilton Square once again.

Upon this humid night, there was no need for the policeman to light his bull's eye lantern, because the silvery light from the full moon in the clear midsummer sky was illuminating every street in Wirral. It was even bright enough to read the fine print of a newspaper. PC Reid inspected the square, then headed up Cleveland Street, where he noticed that his colleague, PC Doyle, was talking to a swaying, singing man leaning on a hansom cab. Constable Reid went to see if his assistance was needed, but discovered that PC Doyle was merely bidding goodnight to a wealthy businessman whom he knew by sight. The drunken man had just stepped down from a cab after a night on the town, and was staggering to his residence with his top hat sitting at a crazy angle.

At twenty minutes past midnight, PC Reid entered Hamilton Square once more, and immediately noticed a light in the second-floor window of one of the houses. He was about to look away when the silhouette of a woman's head and shoulders appeared against the drawn curtains of the lit window, and at the same time he heard a bloodcurdling scream. It was very high-pitched, like the shriek of a child, and was coming from the direction of the house with the illuminated window. PC Reid shuddered when he saw that the silhouetted woman was holding a knife, and she was plunging it repeatedly into something which was out of sight.

He immediately ran over to the house and hammered on the door. After almost two minutes of banging violently on the door knocker and continuously ringing the bell, a light appeared in the semi-circular fanlight window above the front door, and a bolt was drawn back behind that door. A feeble, bent old man answered, and the constable pushed him roughly aside and ran up the stairs, two at a time, stumbling in the dark and was soon on the landing. He opened the door of the drawing room, where he guessed the knife-wielding woman would be. It was a beautifully decorated room, with a thick-piled, royal blue carpet decked with roses, luxurious looking furniture, and an enormous crystal chandelier suspended from the highly decorated plaster ceiling.

Nothing could have prepared PC Reid for the sight that met his eyes when he opened the door to that drawing room, for he had never seen anything as gruesome in all his fourteen years of service. Lolling listlessly in a wine-coloured padded easy chair, was a long-haired woman in a voluminous, full-length white nightgown, which was heavily bloodstained. The woman was staring straight at PC Reid with wide, insane-looking eyes, and she held a long bread knife in her lap. On the floor, was the severed head of a girl of about two years of age, and scattered about the room, were the other bloody body parts of the butchered child.

The woman suddenly came to life as she became aware of the policeman and leapt out of the chair and charged at him with the knife in her hand. Quick as a flash, he pulled the door shut, and he could hear the sound of the blade being stabbed repeatedly into the door panels. By now, the old butler who had admitted Reid was climbing the stairs, as quickly as his old bones would allow, and he too heard the woman screaming and furiously stabbing the drawing room door. PC Reid suddenly noticed that there was a small brass bolt on the door, and he slid it across, effectively locking the murderous woman in the room. The policeman then ordered the elderly servant to leave the premises with him, as his life was in danger. The frail old man protested loudly and PC Reid had to almost carry him outside. He then blew hard on his whistle and PC Doyle quickly responded.

As he hurried to Hamilton Square, Doyle flashed his lantern twice to a policeman on the Laird Street beat, and he came running to the square as well. The three ventured back into the house together. All was now silent and when they entered the drawing room, they found the gas lamps on, as before, but there was no sign of a deranged woman, or of any blood, nor were there any signs of the horrific murder that PC Reid had so graphically described.

PC Reid carefully studied the room; the furniture looked the same as it had before, but the stunning blue carpet was now unaccountably dark green. The old butler, who had wheezed his way back up the stairs yet again, proceeded to tell the officers a strange tale. He explained that he was minding the house until his master returned from a month's holiday in Wales, and that over the past fortnight, he had taken to sleeping with plugs of cottonwool in his ears, because of the awful sounds he had heard coming from the drawing room in the dead of night. Another servant had told him that the sounds were the wails of a ghostly child who was brutally murdered by the master's mentally ill wife some years ago. Apparently, the body was disposed of in secret and the murder hushed up to avoid a scandal. The madwoman had committed suicide not long afterwards, but her ghost had returned to haunt the house. The master had even had a bolt fitted to the outside of the drawing room door to fasten it at night, because that door had been seen to open of its own accord.

The butler offered the policemen a drink but they were so unnerved by the supernatural tale, that they declined the offer and quickly returned to their beats. The Hamilton Square apparition is just one example of instances where the ghost of a murderer, or murder victim, repeatedly goes through the motions of ghastly deeds committed long ago.

REVENGE OF THE MARTHA DUNN

In 1802, a Liverpool clipper, the *Martha Dunn* set sail from Havana to Liverpool, carrying a cargo of two hundred hogsheads of rum and seven hundred sacks of cane sugar. The *Martha Dunn* was captained by William Benedict, a Liverpool-born mariner who had been reared in Pennsylvania. The bond between a captain and his ship is well-known in maritime circles, but Captain Benedict's fondness for the *Martha Dunn* clipper was nothing short of a love affair. The captain frequently paced up and down her decks talking to his vessel, and on some occasions, he would affectionately stroke and pat the ship's bowsprit. The members of the crew were used to their captain's idiosyncrasies, and in a way, they also felt as if the ship had a personality of its own.

A fortnight after leaving Havana, the *Martha Dunn* sailed into Liverpool Bay in the middle of the night. A thick fog was hanging just above the murky waters, and the lookouts could see virtually nothing. All they knew was that they must be close to the Wirral Peninsula. Then one of the lookouts spotted a tiny light flickering in the distance, and assumed that it was the beam of the Mersey lighthouse, guiding them to their destination. The helmsman quickly changed course and Captain Benedict and his crew breathed a huge sigh of relief. Everyone on board assumed that they would soon be berthed at the Salthouse Dock, from where they would head for a well-deserved drink in one of the city's many waterfront taverns.

Minutes after the helmsman had changed course, the rays from the lighthouse flickered, then died away. Too late, Captain Benedict and the crew of the *Martha Dunn* must have realised that the light they had seen had probably come from the lantern of one of the ruthless men known as the 'wreckers'. On nights when visibility was poor, the infamous wreckers lured unsuspecting ships on to the treacherous rocks of the Wallasey coastline, by waving lanterns from the shore, which the sailors mistook for the beams of the lighthouse.

Their dastardly trick certainly worked upon this foggy night, because the *Martha Dunn* soon smashed into the jagged rocks and almost capsized. Captain Benedict and all of the crewmen were thrown into the sea. Three of the crew drowned almost immediately, for, like many sailors of that time, they were unable to swim, and one man's back was fatally broken as he was hurled on to the rocks. Only Captain Benedict and one member of his crew managed to swim to land, but as soon as they reached the pebbled foreshore, the exhausted men were viciously clubbed to death by one of the wreckers. Maritime law stated that a ship could not be legally salvaged if her captain, or even just one of her crew survived, so the wreckers always made sure that there were no survivors.

The band of wreckers who murdered Captain Benedict and his crew belonged to a particularly callous and organised gang of men, who were looked after by a notorious old woman known as 'Mother Redcap', who kept an inn of ill repute on the edge of Liscard Moor. Mother Redcap's inn provided a hiding place for the wreckers and smugglers of Wallasey; a place to stash their loot and hide away from the eyes of the law and the customs officers.

Upon this still and fog-bound night, something very curious happened. As the wreckers rowed out towards the stricken *Martha Dunn*, ready to claim her valuable cargo of rum and sugar, a wind suddenly began to stir. The strengthening breeze quickly wafted away the thick fog and filled out the *Martha Dunn's* magnificent sails. As it did so, the clipper's timbers started to groan and creak, as it backed off the rocks and before long it had righted itself, having reached the open water.

The frustrated wreckers in the lifeboat then watched in amazement, as the deserted ship sailed out to sea. They rowed furiously in an attempt to catch up with her, but it was no use; the *Martha Dunn* was rapidly picking up speed, as the wind which had come from nowhere got behind her sails and blew her out into Liverpool Bay.

Henry Hargreaves, the evil character who had bludgeoned Captain Benedict and his crewman to death, cursed and raged as he watched his valuable prize disappearing before his very eyes. He urged his companions in the lifeboat to keep on rowing after the derelict ship, but they refused, arguing that the wind was too strong and the water too choppy.

At first light, Henry Hargreaves and five of his cronies spotted the *Martha Dunn* sailing erratically in the direction of Hilbre Island, off West Kirby, and they decided to take a small, single-masted fishing vessel out to the clipper, in one last attempt to salvage her. This would prove to be their undoing.

In full view of the crowds who had gathered on the shoreline to watch the salvage operation, the *Martha Dunn* suddenly performed a steady and seemingly controlled U-turn, as if someone was at her wheel. She then started to build up speed and was soon heading rapidly towards the fishing vessel. Henry Hargreaves cringed in sheer terror, as the clipper came careering past the fishing boat. Although it just missed hitting it by a matter of feet, the wake from it almost swamped the tiny vessel.

The two seamen with Hargreaves were beside themselves with fear and claimed that the *Martha Dunn* was possessed and insisted that the chief wrecker return them to land. However, Hargreaves was, above all else, a greedy man, and the thought of someone else claiming the clipper's valuable cargo was too much for him to bear. He cursed his craven shipmates, calling them superstitious, yellow-bellied cowards. Minutes afterwards, the *Martha Dunn*, having executed a very tight turn, was closing in on the fishing boat once again, and this time she rammed it head on and cut straight through the vessel, splintering her hull into matchwood. One of the wreckers was killed instantly in the collision, and the other one slowly bled to death in the water, with a long wooden splinter impaled in his neck. Henry Hargreaves clung desperately to a small, broken-off length of the fishing boat's mast, and was forced to listen to the grotesque gurglings of the doomed man. He also watched with relief as the accursed clipper finally drifted off into the early morning mist.

As soon as he felt that it was safe to do so, Hargreaves started to swim for the shore. He had not gone more than a few yards, when he noticed that the crowd were jumping up and down and roaring with excitement. The wrecker took one look over his shoulder and his worst fears were confirmed. The towering hulk of the *Martha Dunn* was almost upon him. Hargreaves was briefly heard to scream out as the massive hull smashed into him. His bloated, broken body was later found on the sands of Hoylake; bloated, stinking and rotten, it had been half-eaten by crabs and seagulls.

No one knows what happened to the *Martha Dunn*, but there were many strange tales about her fate. According to one legend, just as the body of Captain Benedict was being buried in a churchyard overlooking the sea near Neston, the deserted ship came floating down the River Dee in full sail, and sank within sight of the startled mourners. It was as if the derelict ship had decided to join her beloved captain in one last supreme act of loyalty ...

EARLY AIR-MAIL?

In March 1856, a strange whistling sound was heard in the early morning skies over Hooton, Wirral. A farmer working in the area by the name of Graves told people that he saw a strange white object drifting high over the far side of his field, and when he went in search of it, he found nothing resembling the object, only a band of mysterious strangers dressed in black, who warned him to keep away from the wood behind them.

A week later, something else fell from the sky on to southern Wirral, about a quarter of a mile south of Hooton. At seven o'clock in the morning, an old woman at Childer Thornton heard a thunderous explosion in the garden of her cottage, and when she went outside to find out what had caused the blast, she found pieces of metal and shredded paper scattered everywhere. Unfortunately, the old woman was illiterate, and so was unable to make head or tail of the torn scraps of the documents which had landed on her property.

Stranger still, a group of men who claimed to be detectives later turned up at the cottage and painstakingly collected all the scraps of paper and fragments of metal, down to the last minute pieces. It was as if an artillery shell, stuffed with a bundle of papers, had exploded on impact with the ground.

A month later, another mysterious projectile whistled at a hypersonic velocity towards the north of Wirral, and it came from the direction of Bootle. Fishermen on the Wallasey coast saw something plunge into the sea and throw up a great plume of spray.

Mysterious explosions have been heard in other parts of the world. Throughout the nineteenth century, deafening booms of unknown origin were heard regularly throughout the Ganges Delta in India, and were nicknamed the Guns of Barisal (a port in the Bay of Bengal).

Closer to home, the sailors of the Mersey were well aware of the equally mysterious 'mist pouffers' – uncanny thundering sounds which came from nowhere and bombarded their ears in the middle of the ocean. Most of the sailors at Liverpool docks and the inhabitants of the Wirral who had heard the strange explosions and whistling sounds in 1856, thought that they were some kind of supernatural phenomenon, but the truth seems to be somewhat more mundane, but intriguing nevertheless.

In 1856, brilliant Mancunian, Joseph Whitworth, was building various mortars, cannons and military guns at the Vauxhall foundry in Liverpool. On 6 May 1856, Whitworth had his giant hexagonal gun rolled down to the shore at Bootle, in order to show it off to the assembled members of the military. A twenty-four-pound metal ball was fired, but went off course in its trajectory and came down in Waterloo, where it sliced through a tree, before entering the parlour window of a merchant named Houghton. The cannon ball scattered the merchant's furniture and impacted into an internal wall, but by a miracle, no one was injured.

John Jones, another genius working with Whitworth at the time, had a grand plan to put letters and parcels into a shell-shaped cartridge that could be fired across the Mersey to the Wirral peninsula. Such 'ballistic mail' would almost be as fast as a modern email. However, unlike email, the mail delivered by Whitworth's gun would have the advantage of being able to include parcels. A parachute would possibly have been deployed once the shell had traversed a given distance on its parabolic path, to ensure that its cargo arrived intact.

Could all this explain the strange projectiles that fell on Wirral in 1856, scattering bits of metal and scraps of paper in their wake?

MYSTERIES OF THE DEEP

A visitor from another world would probably find it strange that we call our planet 'Earth', when, in fact, over two-thirds of the planet's surface area is submerged under water. The vast oceans that cover the Earth are mostly unexplored, due to the difficulties and dangers associated with deep sea diving, and there are undoubtedly many unknown sea creatures living in their depths that marine biologists have yet to discover.

In 1938, a large fish called the Coelacanth was caught in the Indian Ocean. The huge, fearsome-looking fish, which was swimming the seas when the dinosaurs ruled the Earth, was thought to have become extinct seventy millions of years ago. If it managed to survive the age of the dinosaurs, it must be possible that even larger creatures have also survived and are perhaps still be roaming the ocean bed?

As late as 1991, Smithsonian and Peruvian scientists described a new species of beaked whale that had previously gone undetected in the oceans of the world. New discoveries of various species of sea creature are regularly made, and some think that the Loch Ness Monster and the sea serpents of old maritime folklore, may have a basis in fact. In this part of the world, there have been numerous well-documented encounters with unidentified sea creatures, and many of the incidents took place in Merseyside and Wirral waters.

In the 1880s, on several occasions, fishermen spotted a long, snake-like creature, with eleven humps, cruising from the River Dee towards Liverpool Bay. A Justice of the Peace from Liverpool, vacationing in Llandudno in 1882, sighted the same humped 'sea monster' and later signed an affidavit stating that it was over three hundred feet in length, and was swimming out towards Liverpool Bay. Eight other people walking along the promenade at Llandudno also saw the same large creature.

For centuries, fishermen in Cardigan Bay have claimed that a sea serpent, which they call Morgwar, patrols the Irish Sea. Curiously, the Cornish fishermen also call their legendary sea monster Morgwar. Legend has it that Morgwar belonged to a race of monsters from the north, and that one of these serpents – also referred to as a dragon – had a lair in a riverside cave. According to some mediaeval maps, this cave was located close to modern day Ellesmere Port. In the days of King Arthur, Sir Gawain, an outstanding Knight of the Round Table, set off to slay the monster, which was causing havoc with the local fishing community. He chased it into what is now Delamere Forest and there he slayed it.

In modern times there have been a few alleged encounters with a spine-chilling creature at West Kirby, which have usually been explained away as figments of the imagination and urban legend, but I am not so sure.

The first report comes from thirteen-year-old Susan

Rogers, from Liverpool, who was visiting Hilbre Island in the winter of 1954 with her eighteen-year-old cousin, Tina Jones. Susan had had a row with Tina whilst walking on the island and in a sulk she ran off to hide. Tina searched everywhere for her cousin and repeatedly shouted out to her, warning her that the tide would soon be coming in, leaving the island cut off from the mainland, and they would have to spend the night there.

Meanwhile, Susan had flounced off into the 'Ladies' Cave' on the island, as the rain-laden skies turned ever gloomier. She was peeping out from the entrance to see if Tina was looking for her – when she became aware of an unusual rattling sound. At first she thought the sound was just the pattering of rain on the rocks, as the skies opened and there was a sudden downpour. Then something rough touched the girl's bare ankle, making her jump. She looked down and saw what looked like a dark brown length of cane covered with stiff bristles, quivering between her sandals. She spun round and was met by something truly mind-blowing.

Emerging from the dark recesses of the cave was a gigantic crustacean, about four feet high and six feet wide, and standing on four, perhaps even six, jointed legs. The monster was grey in colour and was clad in an armour of hard segmented shells, but the most frightening thing about it was the pair of massive blood-red eyes which swivelled around in its head.

Susan almost passed out with fear.

The strange, bristled cane-like thing, which was now prodding at her skirt, turned out to be one of two antennae that were attached to the head of the monstrosity. Its mouth clacked opened and closed with a rattling sound and its legs clicked and clattered on the rocks as it scrabbled towards her. Susan leapt from the cave mouth and landed awkwardly on the seaweed-strewn, rain-slicked rocks below, twisting her ankle painfully. She still couldn't scream – her vocal cords seemed to be paralysed – and she almost blacked out twice as she scrambled across the beach, because she could still hear the ominous clattering of the beast behind her.

Tina found her in a very sorry state, cowering behind a boulder, crouched on all fours and as pale as death. She shuddered when Susan told her about the 'thing' in the cave and she pulled her away and helped her hobble back to the mainland. They only just made it, because by the time they reached the shoreline, the water was lapping round their ankles. Any longer, and the rapidly incoming tide would have swept them off their feet.

The mysterious shelled creature was allegedly seen on several more occasions at Hilbre Island in the 1960s, and there is even one report of a similar creature being washed ashore on Parkgate promenade, during a fierce storm in the late 1940s. Men delivering beer to a waterfront pub said the crab-like creature was some seven feet in length, and it kicked furiously on its back until a wave crashed over the promenade and righted it. The weird-looking creature then scuttled sideways back into the sea.

A *Liverpool Echo* newspaper clipping I received from a reader about a waterfront junk yard in northern Liverpool, in the 1970s, described how two junkmen were clearing out part of their yard when they spotted a brown-skinned creature burrowing beneath a mound of rusting scrap. It looked something like an octopus, with very long thin tentacles. Some of the scrap metal parts at the bottom of the heap dated back to the 1940s, and had lain undisturbed for years, and it appeared that it had fashioned its lair beneath all the junk. The two junkmen could hear something moving about and breathing "like a pair of bellows" beneath the scrap pile, and they even called for assistance to remove the rusting heap from two mechanics from a nearby garage.

Night soon fell, and the scrap was finally removed by the light from a fire in a brazier and a homemade torch made from a paraffin-soaked cloth tied to a length of pipe. There was a hole, nine inches across, in the yard floor, where the scrap had been piled, and peering from this hole was an eye of some sort. The four men jumped back in horror when a thin, worm-like tentacle slithered out and tried to drag a chunk of an old car alternator over the hole to reseal it. The burning torch was thrust at the tentacle, and one of the junkyard men brought an air rifle from his hut and fired a .22 slug down the hole. The creature let out a faint squeal of pain and moments later, another similar sound was heard coming from a sewer grid in the street just outside the junkyard. The creature had literally gone to ground.

I mentioned this case on the radio and two people telephoned to say that they had worked in a junkyard in 1975 and remembered hearing about the weird creature under the scrap-yard. When the yard was later excavated to make way for the building of a new premises, a slick of grease and oil that had filtered down from the scrap over the years had formed, and in this layer of greasy mulch, the remains of what looked like a huge decomposed jellyfish was found. Unfortunately, no marine biologist was called for to examine the remains. The Philistine workers simply tossed the mysterious creature into a skip.

THE AXE MAN
OF BEBINGTON MILL

Tom Walker now lives in Australia, but when he was a child growing up in Bebington, he lived in mortal fear of a weird and extremely agile ghost that haunted Bebington Mill in the early 1960s. The cone-shaped, semi-derelict tower of the mill seemed deserted to Tom, but things were often seen to be moving behind the black squares of the rotted window frames on each of the building's three storeys. Tom often roamed the area surrounding the mill in the company of a small gang of friends. Their leader was a wild fourteen-year-old named Jack, whose main ambition in life seemed to be to cause as much disruption as possible in the lives of the citizens of Bebington.

One summer night, Jack noticed a figure peering out from the empty top window frame of Bebington Mill, and drew the gang's attention to it. Tom was wary and warned him that he had heard that the mill was haunted, but Jack took no notice; it was his job to appear fearless at all times. Swaggering up to the foot of the mill, he shouted up to the thing peering out through the dilapidated window, "Hey! You! Are you spying on us, or something? We'll come up there and throw you out the window, if you don't watch it!"

The gang of five laughed nervously as the figure moved away from the window ledge into the dark interior of the mill, only to reappear in another window on the next floor some moments later, this time angrily waving his fist. He seemed to have a head of long white hair.

"Let's go, Jack," urged Tom Walker, his voice betraying a deep sense of unease.

"He's just some old tramp," Jack declared, with his usual swagger. "We'll give him a good kicking."

The gang members held back and waited to see what their leader would do next. Jack looked about him and was just about to pick up a three-foot length of wood, when the man with the long white hair suddenly reappeared at the foot of the mill. Dressed in a bib and brace, he was wielding a long-handled axe and came charging towards the gang. Forgetting his street cred, Jack swore loudly and ran off, leaving the gang to fend for themselves. They quickly followed suit and as Tom shoved one of the lads out of the way to make his escape, the axe whistled past his head. Miraculously, it landed in a hedge to his right, without hitting any of the fleeing youngsters. The man continued to pursue the boys, letting out a string of filthy expletives and obscene insults. Tom was brave enough to sneak one backward glance at their pursuer, and saw the white-haired madman springing along like a gazelle, even though he appeared to be at least sixty.

Jack must have possessed amazing powers of persuasion, because, despite the previous day's cowardly retreat, he managed to coax them all back to the old mill the very next evening, where once again he started to taunt the elderly axe-man into making an appearance. On this occasion, the gang members scattered as soon as the old man appeared, but Jack tripped over a stone in the retreat, which left him sprawled on the ground and very vulnerable. The sprightly old man quickly caught up with him and proceeded to kick him viciously in the stomach. Jack was defenceless against the attack, and had resigned himself to being seriously injured or even killed, when, after the third kick, the unexpected happened and the attacker vanished right before his eyes.

Many years later, when Tom Walker was an adult, he bumped into his old friend Jack on a cruise ship, and the two men began reminiscing about their childhood adventures. When Tom mentioned the ghost of Bebington Mill, Jack's face turned pale, and he said, "For years I told myself that I had imagined that old man, but the bruises were real enough."

"No, you didn't imagine him, Jack," Tom told him. "He was as real as you or me. We all saw him."

The identity of the white-haired ghost, which gave a bunch of young tearaways a taste of their own medicine, remains a complete mystery.

SENTRIES OF STONE

In the school holidays of the blistering summer of 1976, three youngsters from Merseyside went to stay with their relatives in North Wales. They were thirteen-year-old Morgana Phillips from Warbreck Moor in Aintree, fourteen-year-old Roger Fray of Granby Street, Toxteth, and thirteen-year-old Phillip Donnelly from Hoylake. All three were related, and they went to stay with aunty and uncle living near the Whitford area of Flintshire, near Holywell.

The three Merseyside teenagers were made very welcome in Wales and were beside themselves with excitement about what they regarded as an adventure away from their parents. Once they had unpacked all their things and had a snack, they were ready to explore their new surroundings. They were just going out of the door when their aunt stopped them, "Just before you go, my dears, erm ... there's something I need to tell you ... something important."

"Okay, promise we won't talk to any strangers, Auntie Gwen," sighed Roger, "and if we see the big bad wolf, we'll run back home!" he added sarcastically, looking across to the others for their reaction.

"Very funny!" said Aunt Gwen. "But, seriously, there's a field about a mile away in that direction," Gwen said, pointing in an area west of the cottage. "Down that lane, across the stream, past the derelict farm to the crossroads. You must not go anywhere near it. I don't want to have to tell your parents that you've come to any harm."

"Why, what's going to happen to us if we do?" asked Phillip, trying to sound polite, as he didn't want to upset Auntie Gwen.

"Well, in the middle of the field there's a tall stone cross called the Stone of Lamentations. Nobody from these parts goes anywhere near it. It's said to be protected by very dark forces."

"Oh, come on, Auntie Gwen. You don't really believe in all that rubbish, do you?"

"You can laugh, but I'm not the only one. No one in the village ever goes there any more."

Gwen's face remained stern.

"Okay, if it makes you happy, we won't go there," said Phillip, nudging the others. "Come on, you two, let's get out of Auntie Gwen's way."

Of course, being the age they were, the minute their aunt had closed the door, the children's appetites for adventure having been whetted, they deliberately set out to find the forbidden field and the curious Stone of Lamentations. As they ran down the lane, they laughed about their Auntie Gwen's ludicrous 'dark forces' and chased after each other making ghostly noises and shouting, "The dark forces are after you!" in exaggerated Welsh accents.

When they reached the crossroads they had little difficulty in locating the field she had described. Along two of its sides ran the two roads, at right angles to one another. On the other two sides there was thick forest, which seemed to stretch for miles in both directions. And there, right up in the far corner, was the mediaeval stone cross, and, to their surprise, there seemed to be someone standing by the foot of it.

The mischievous trio suddenly lost all their bravado, but, egged on by each other, they climbed over the stile and made their way up to the cross. By the time they got there, they had all become completely subdued, and each was secretly wishing that they had taken their aunt's advice and stayed away.

There was indeed someone standing by the monument; an elderly, scruffily-dressed man with a huge unruly white beard, leaning very close to the base of the lichen-encrusted cross, apparently trying to decipher the strange symbols and drawings carved into it. At his side was a grey-nosed, sad-looking Labrador, standing guard over the old man's paltry possessions – various scruffy bundles tied together with bits of string, and a long, faded, green canvas bag. The pair were not in any way frightening, just rather incongruous in such an isolated spot.

The three curious teenagers gathered around the man, who eventually turned and introduced himself as Mr Hopkins and then asked their names. They all sat down at the base of the monument, where he related a breath-taking tale that was perfectly true. For as long as people could remember, it had been claimed that a very important piece of treasure was buried in the field near to the stone cross. Naturally, over the years, this had brought many people flocking to the field, armed with trowels and spades and, later, metal detectors. Not only had all the treasure seekers failed to find the fabled treasure, but many of them had been struck by bolts of lightning in the middle of their labours – even on beautiful summer days, when the sky was clear of all clouds.

Mr Hopkins admitted that he had also come in search of the treasure, but he was not afraid. He wore a special talisman called the Seal of Solomon, which, he maintained, would prevent him from being struck down, but even so, his task would be far from easy. He still had one problem to overcome before he could lay his hands on the legendary treasure. He told them that from the cover of the sprawling forest all around the field, ghostly figures on horseback had been seen to ride on certain nights when the moon was full. The figures were said to be clad in strange armour, and their helmets were horned like the ones reputedly worn by the Vikings. Each of the phantom horsemen was also armed with a bow and arrows. People had reported seeing these apparitions for years, but no one knew whose ghosts they were, or where they came from.

Mr Hopkins said he had studied all of the folklore and obscure history of Wales for many years, and he had come to the conclusion that the ghostly riders were the sentries who guarded the Stone of Lamentations. If just one of their arrows struck a living person, anywhere on the body, that person would drop dead immediately. The three captivated teenagers shuddered as he added that, even at that moment, he could feel the ancient eyes of the sentries upon him.

"They are watching from the forest right now," he said, nervously looking about him. "They can sense what I am after."

His words filled the youngsters with a sense of foreboding, and they too cast anxious glances towards the forest, and instinctively huddled closer together. The old man, however, proceeded to bravely pitch his ragged little one-man tent near the forest's edge, while his dog sat, ears pricked, watching and listening. As he worked, puffing and panting with the exertion, Mr Hopkins told the children not to tell anyone he was staying there – he didn't want anybody interfering with his plan.

His tent securely pitched, he squatted down in front of it and consulted an old almanac which confirmed that the moon would be full when it rose that night. He then produced the long green canvas bag, from which he took a gleaming, polished shotgun. He stroked the barrel of the sleek weapon, which was obviously his pride and joy, and announced that his intention was to shoot as many of the ghostly riders as he could, if they chose to put in an appearance that night.

"I read somewhere that ghosts can't be shot," said Morgana. "Are you sure you'll be safe here on your own?"

"Don't you worry, missy," replied Mr Hopkins. "These apparitions are not the usual type of ghost you might meet in a haunted house – they're the product of a long-dead wizard's black magic. The ammunition in this shotgun has been made from a silver crucifix that has been blessed with holy water. The hallowed ammunition will destroy the evil apparitions, and the treasure will no longer then be guarded. You mark my words."

Phillip Donnelly asked just what the treasure was supposed to be, and Mr Hopkins said he believed – from reading and interpreting the arcane drawings on the stone – that it was Merlin's Sceptre; a gilded staff said to have been brought from Atlantis aeons ago. Such staffs, Hopkins stated, had been used to build Stonehenge and the great pyramids in Egypt.

That night, a full moon rose, bathing the landscape in a bright silvery blue that was almost electric, and Hopkins sat before a dying wood fire that glowed with an orange incandescence. His dog, exhausted by the day's events, was curled up next to him, enjoying the warmth. After returning for supper, the three teenagers had managed to slip away from their aunt and uncle's home and Morgana Phillips was still wearing her pyjamas and slippers.

They sat feeding twigs into the fire's feeble flames, when an owl hooted from somewhere in the forest's black depths, followed by a long, strained silence. Then Hopkin's dog suddenly leapt to its feet and let out a long, mournful howl. They heard what sounded like a horn, quickly followed by the rumble of horses' hooves. Morgana and the two boys were terrified, and took refuge behind the old man, the three of them squashed inside the tiny tent.

Hopkins sprang to his feet and took up his position, ready to fire the shotgun. Morgana screamed as the first ghostly figure emerged from the inky blackness of the forest. It was clad in hefty armour and gave off a faint red glow like St Elmo's Fire. It aimed its bow at Hopkins, but before it could release its deadly arrow, the shotgun discharged its ammunition, and the silver bullet blasted the evil spectre, which evaporated in an instant, along with the red-eyed horse.

Two more figures on horseback thundered out from the shadows and the second blast from Hopkins' shotgun caught them both at once and dispatched them to oblivion. While the shotgun was being reloaded, a pale green arrow whizzed within an inch of Roger's knee and hit the Labrador's hind quarters. It yelped just once and fell down dead, yet the arrow vanished the instant it hit the animal.

The shotgun blasted out again, and another rider

vanished, along with its horse. Morgana caught a glimpse of one of the armoured horsemen's faces, and saw that it was not a face at all, but a skull, hideous and with hollow, burning red eyes. The shotgun was discharged again, and the remaining four horsemen pulled up their steeds and turned and rode back from whence they came – deep into the dark depths of the forest. They did not return that night.

At dawn, the children watched in silence as Hopkins buried his faithful old dog. Then Roger, Phillip and Morgana went home, sneaking in through the kitchen door and creeping to their beds. Not one of them slept a wink – the awful events of the night playing over and over again in their fevered minds. However, their taste for adventure was undeterred, and they returned to the field at around one o'clock in the afternoon, only to find the old man sitting by a blazing fire, skinning a rabbit, as calm as could be. Nearby was his sacred ammunition, all packed away ready for the next encounter with the evil sentries on horseback.

After chatting for a while, and marvelling at the old man's courage and survival skills, the three youngsters wandered off into the forest – not too far, and always keeping the field in sight – and there they came upon an amazing find. Lying on the ground was an old horn – about eighteen inches long – elaborately carved out of bone. It had graven spirals and strange Celtic designs etched upon it. They all agreed that one of the sentries must have dropped it the night before, during the chaotic retreat.

Without thinking, Phillip Donnelly picked up the horn, and blew into it. It made a strange low sound that reverberated through the forest. Almost immediately, the ground started to shake. Then, seemingly out of nowhere, and this time in broad daylight, there came six dark figures on galloping horses. The horn had obviously summoned them. The three of them ran for their lives as a shower of arrows zipped past them. They came crashing out of the forest, startling Mr Hopkins, who was roasting his rabbit on a spit he had fashioned from tree branches. He stood up and asked, "What's going on?"

Before any of them could answer, Hopkins heard, then saw, the sentries come hurtling out of the dark green shadows of the forest into the daylight. He hadn't bargained on an attack before nightfall and realised that he wouldn't be able to load his shotgun in time. So he ran. Surprisingly agile for his age, he was running closely behind the fleeing teenagers when there was a loud and sickening thud. An arrow had hit him squarely in the back. The old man's body was felled instantly and rolled to a halt in the tall grass.

Morgana and the two boys briefly looked back and saw the old man fall. As soon as the horsemen had hit the old man, they had turned and galloped back into the forest, but the youngsters were too frightened for their own lives to go back and look after their friend. So fast did they run the mile back to their aunt's house, that they had no energy left to speak by the time they reached the cottage.

Gwen got the shock of her life when they burst through the door, and collapsed, gasping, on to the sofa. "What on earth's the matter with you three?" she asked. "You look like you've seen a ghost."

"Oh, Auntie Gwen, you're not going to believe this," said Roger when he finally summoned enough breath, "but we'll tell you anyway."

The three of them then babbled out their story. Even though it was she who had warned them about the field and the stone cross the day before, for some reason, Gwen could not bring herself to believe their incredible story. When her husband came home, he, too, poured scorn on their story, as did their neighbours on both sides, who treated the rumours which circulated in the neighbourhood as fanciful nonsense.

"City kids!" said one of them. "They see a bit of countryside and go mad. Somebody's been filling their heads with a lot of rubbish," she added, giving Gwen a meaningful look.

On the following morning, the papers merely stated that an old poacher, who was a bit of a local character, had died of a heart attack and had been found in the field by the crossroads. What made the story more newsworthy was the fact that the grave of his dog had also been found, just outside his tent. When the dog's body was disinterred, the vet could find no cause of death.

So it seems that the treasure then, if indeed it exists at all, is still unclaimed.

This story was related to me by the people who experienced the incredible events at first hand. They are now adults, and they swear that everything in the story really did take place. I have visited the Stone of Lamentations myself, and also the nearby forest, and although I am not psychic, I had the uncanny sensation that something in the locality was watching me.

People who live in the area also told me of many strange and unnatural deaths that have occurred in the vicinity of the stone over the years, including the freak accident in which a pair of lovers were zapped by a bolt of lightning from a clear blue sky in the 1970s. They survived the strike, but the searing heat caused the skin on the palms of their hands to stick together, as they were walking along hand in hand. Surgery was required to separate them.

In 1995, an American tourist spotted the stone cross as he approached the crossroads. He was intrigued by its position, in a field, away from all habitation, and he set off to take a closer look. He felt something hard slam into his chest as he was crossing the field, halfway between the stile and the stone cross. With enormous force, the invisible projectile knocked him on to his back, and he subsequently discovered a small round hole in the left breast pocket of his jacket, which had also penetrated his wallet.

A DEAD MAN HANGS

In the early summer of 1977 there were several reports of a figure that was seen running into the River Dee, only to vanish without so much as a splash. A Liverpool family witnessed this strange spectacle, and it was even mentioned on the local Radio City news programme. Perhaps the following story will throw some light on the strange river-bound ghost.

On May Day in 1801, John Clare, a young man in his twenties, put a handkerchief over the lower half of his face and secreted himself inside a bush outside a cottage on the outskirts of Chester. Night was falling fast, and as he gently fondled the blade of the knife he was holding, he watched an old woman wearing a bonnet leave her house to travel the short distance to her sister's home, less than half a mile away. He was not surprised by this, because it was common knowledge in the neighbourhood that she did this every Friday night. The old woman, Mrs Keel, was an eccentric who was rumoured to practise witchcraft, but what interested John Clare, was the fortune in savings that old Mrs Keel was supposed to have hidden under her bed.

As soon as the old woman had locked her door and trotted off into the gathering dusk, John Clare kicked down the door of her cottage and ransacked the place from top to bottom. He crawled right under the bed and felt under every one of the iron springs. His prying fingers probed every nook and cranny, but he didn't manage to find anything of value, except for a few dusty coins at the bottom an old vase.

Before leaving the cottage, in a fit of frustration, he started throwing things about and smashing anything which came to hand. His feelings vented at last, he stomped towards the door, but was taken aback when he found his way barred by an enormous, black Labrador dog that sat squarely across the doorway and seemed to have appeared out of nowhere. The dog was glaring intently at him with a pair of very uncanny-looking eyes. John Clare shouted at the hound, but it didn't flinch. He was just considering climbing out of the cottage by a side window, when he suddenly heard a voice calling out to the dog. It got up and padded away, to reveal old Mrs Keel, standing in the doorway. Her grey, steely eyes shot right through the young burglar, who, having been caught red-handed, was now brandishing his knife in panic.

"Get out of my way, old woman, or you'll be done to death," he screamed, hoping to intimidate her.

"I'm a Romany woman," replied Mrs Keel, fixing Clare with her cold grey eyes, "and by threatening me you have sealed your doom."

John Clare laughed nervously and waved his knife at her, saying, "Nonsense, get out of my way, you old crone."

But Mrs Keel gave him the fright of his life when she addressed him again and this time she spoke his name, "Take heed, John Clare, they will hang you after you kill yourself," she said.

John Clare was taken aback by this seemingly absurd statement. Backed into a corner, he decided that he now had no alternative; he would have to kill the old woman, as she had somehow found out his name, but just as he was lunging towards her, the black dog made a sudden reappearance, this time with teeth bared. It chased him out of the house, snapping at his heels.

The hapless burglar then took refuge in the local forest, in order to take stock of his situation. The events of that night had left him feeling very jittery and vulnerable and he decided to leave the Chester area as soon as he could gather together a few possessions. As he was attempting to put his plan into action the next day, he was spotted by the sheriff and brought into custody, where Mrs Keel soon identified him. In 1801, murder was not the only crime that carried the death penalty; people were hanged for burglary and even for stealing loaves of bread. John Clare had not only committed burglary, but had also threatened his victim with a knife. Punishments were short and swift and he was sentenced to hang on Saturday, 9 May, of that same year.

As he languished in his cramped prison cell, the condemned man hatched a desperate escape plan. He knew that the cart that was to take him to Gallows Hill would stop at a point near the River Dee and he planned to make a break for freedom as soon as he was untied as the cart neared the gallows. He knew the riverbank very well at that point and believed that he could shake off anyone pursuing him without any difficulty.

On the Saturday morning of his execution, John Clare had his wrists bound with rope and hefty leg irons were fastened to him at his ankles. He was bundled into a cart along with two forgers named Thompson and Morgan. As the cart trundled off to the scene of what was billed to be a triple public execution, Clare started smiling to himself, and to the people lining the route hoping to catch a glimpse of the doomed villains, he called out, "They will never hang me, you'll see!"

As the cart rumbled on, one of the other condemned men became so terrified by the thought of his impending fate, that he was physically sick. The other man started to cry, but John Clare simply laughed at them both and waved to the crowds as if they were going on a picnic.

The cart finally rattled to a halt at Gallows Hill, where hundreds of bloodthirsty spectators were waiting to see the three men hang. In those days, a good hanging was something to be eagerly anticipated, a break from the monotony and drudgery of everyday life – and so a triple hanging was even better. Among the spectators, standing right at the back of the crowd, stood old Mrs Keel, wearing a large, black hood.

One of the condemned men fainted at the foot of the gallows, and had to be carried up the wooden steps by two men who seemed to find the proceedings very amusing, and laughed and joked about the state of their inert captive. The other forger was grabbed by the sheriff's men, as he pleaded, "I'm just a forger. I haven't done anybody any real harm. I don't deserve this. Please have mercy on me!"

"You'll be nothing but dead meat soon," quipped one of the sheriff's men, manhandling him up the steps, which brought chortles of laughter from some members of the mob.

Meanwhile, John Clare stood calmly in the cart, awaiting his moment. Eventually they came for him and his wrists were untied. As soon as his hands were free, he punched the sheriff's man hard in the face and sent him hurtling off the side of the cart and into the crowd. In the confusion, as the mob roared with laughter at this unexpected twist in their day's entertainment, John Clare launched himself off the side of the cart, and immediately screamed with pain, because he had somehow overlooked the heavy leg irons, which were shackled to his ankles. Undeterred, the young tearaway continued with his desperate bid for freedom, but felt as if he was running in slow motion with the heavy irons painfully chafing his ankle bones and dramatically slowing his progress.

The crowd surged after him, and so did the sheriff's men, who found the whole episode hilarious and were now in hysterics. Hobbled as he was, John Clare soon toppled over, and rolled down the steep bank out of control – towards the River Dee. He plunged into the swift-flowing waters, where he frantically tried to swim over to the opposite bank, but the irons were like a dead weight, and he sank to the bottom and drowned.

Throughout this drama, an old woman in a black hood was cackling with laughter on the top of the riverbank as she looked down at the terrified face beneath the waters. A wide-eyed, terror-stricken John Clare was looking up at her with the last bubbles of air escaping from his mouth.

Then the hunt was on to find his corpse and the crowd scurried along the banks of the Dee, each person desperate to be the first to spot the corpse. Their efforts were soon to be rewarded. Just one hour later, John Clare's livid corpse was recovered from the river, and carried back to the gallows. With unnecessary cruelty, Thompson and Morgan were forced to watch as the limp, dripping body was hanged without the traditional hood on its head. They too were then hanged, as the crowd of men women and children looked on and cheered.

Old Mrs Keel's strange prediction had come to pass – John Clare had indeed been hanged after he had killed himself by jumping into the river. That night, Mrs Keel was seen standing in the moonlight, coolly surveying the body of John Clare, as it dangled grotesquely from the gibbet. And beside Mrs Keel sat her huge, impassive, black, Labrador dog.

AND THE BEAT GOES ON

This is a creepy story about something which happened around Halloween, in 1999, when residents at a block of flats in Birkenhead complained to their housing association about their new noisy neighbour on the top floor, who, every night, would play Motown songs continuously from 8 o'clock, into the early hours of the morning. Residents had tried banging on his door to complain, but the music seemed to mysteriously die down whenever anyone approached the flat, as if teasing the complainant. None of the residents knew who the new and unwelcome addition to their block was, but they had often heard him walking down the communal stairs at 2 o'clock in the morning, whistling loudly and waking everybody up.

Staff at the housing association dealing with the complaints were baffled, because, according to their books, the flat where the noisy resident lived was unoccupied. Assuming that a squatter had moved into the empty premises, two officers from the association went to the flats to investigate. When they entered the flat in question, they found it completely empty and in exactly the same unoccupied state it had been in since the previous occupant had died, two months back.

Now for the really weird part. As the two housing officers left the flat, and headed for the stairs, loud music began blaring out from the empty dwelling. It was that old sixties song, 'The Midnight Hour', by Wilson Pickett. The officers stopped in their tracks and looked at each other in disbelief. They couldn't just ignore it after all the complaints, so they reluctantly returned to the flat. As soon as they entered the hallway, the music mysteriously faded away. Seconds later, the two officers heard footsteps pass by them and leave the flat by the front door. At first, they wondered whether the inexplicable footsteps had just been in their imagination, until two residents came out of their flats and claimed to have also heard the phantom footsteps going down the flights of steps at the same time.

So what could have been behind all this musical mayhem? Well, it has since been established that, in 1996 – more than thirty years before all this took place – a previous tenant of the haunted flat had died of a heart attack whilst on the premises. Much to the annoyance of his neighbours, this man had often played Motown songs on his record player, late into the night and at full blast. Older residents also told how this same man used to annoy everybody by always whistling loudly as he walked down the stairs, as if to announce his presence.

So it seems that the cause of the footsteps can now be determined, but only through a supernatural explanation …

Strange Apparitions

Not far from Ledsham, there is a winding country lane near the A540, that runs from Puddington to the celebrated Ness Gardens. This road is said to be haunted by a peculiarly sinister ghost – the phantom of a motorcyclist who has his head on the wrong way round! The origin of this tale is said to be in a tragic accident that allegedly took place on the road in the 1930s. A man named Hatherton used to drive his motorcycle and sidecar up and down the lane regularly as he visited his sweetheart – the daughter of a Burton farmer. One bitterly cold night, she let Hatherton borrow her brother's coat, but it was a bit too small, and he couldn't button it up properly because it was so tight. The girl fussed round her boyfriend and advised him to put the coat on back to front, so that the freezing cold, knife-edged wind would not give him pleurisy.

So Hatherton put the coat on back to front, kissed his girlfriend, and rode off through the wintry night. At a sharp bend in the road the bike and its sidecar slid out of control, on black ice and smashed into a tree. A slow-witted but brawny farm labourer came upon the wreckage, and found Hatherton lying unconscious, face down in the ditch. The bike and the wreckage of the sidecar were covering his legs. The boy did not realise that the coat was being worn back to front. He thought the driver's neck was broken, and when he heard Hatherton moaning, he made a desperate attempt to twist his head the right way round. In so doing, he achieved what the accident had failed to do, and snapped Hatherton's spinal chord.

Not long afterwards, people travelling on that stretch of

road after dark reported seeing a motorcycle and sidecar being driven by a man with his head twisted around through 180 degrees.

❋ ❋ ❋ ❋

A ghost that is arguably stranger still, is said to haunt a certain street in Birkenhead, where an old club once stood. The club used to showcase variety acts, but was eventually demolished and new houses now stand on the spot, so I have to be careful, as I don't want to frighten the present inhabitants.

In the 1970s, an elderly performer who went under various stage names in the course of his cabaret career, dreamt up a character called Frederick – a six-foot-tall baby in a huge nappy, complete with safety-pin, and an old-fashioned petal-rimmed baby bonnet. With a rattle in his hand, Frederick was about to make his debut on stage, when the comic portraying him dropped dead unexpectedly from a thrombosis of the brain. He died alone and in great agony in the club's dressing room, where he was found lying in a pool of his own blood.

The club was closed for three days as a mark of respect, but when it reopened, a well-known comedy duo, who had never performed at the club before and knew nothing of its recent tragedy, were amused to see a man dressed as a big baby walking around backstage. They asked the management who he was, but were met only with silence and horrified gasps. After the comics had performed their act and been paid, the management told them about the recent tragedy concerning Frederick. The comedy duo were very unhappy about what they had been told and never appeared at that club again.

A singer and comedian who was unlucky enough to

witness the 'big baby' at close quarters, as he was setting up his public address system, said he saw blood gushing down the apparition's face and bubbling from its nose.

As recently as May 2002, Glenys, Patsy and Rob – three residents who live near the spot where the old variety club used to stand – asked me if I had ever heard of the ghost of a man dressed as a baby. I told them about Frederick, and they said that they had seen him looking through the window of a house in the early hours of the morning. At first they thought it was someone playing a prank, but then the figure inexplicably vanished into an alleyway. Patsy mentioned the bizarre-looking ghost to her Special Constable boyfriend, and he admitted that he had also seen the ghost some months back, but had told no one because he was sure that no one would believe him.

THE VILLAGE ON THE CEILING

There are many places which will never feature on our primitive maps, believe me. There are places under our very noses, of which we are as ignorant as a medieval peasant would have been of the craters on the far side of the Moon. Our atlases are two-dimensional representations of known three-dimensional lands on flat paper, and they have their serious limitations. Spreading the surface of the earth's globe on to a piece of flat paper, or a computer screen, inevitably causes major distortions, because we are attempting to reduce three dimensions to two – which is physically impossible.

Physicists today suspect that there are many more dimensions than the usual three spatial ones (length, breadth and height) to which we are accustomed, and that there may be undiscovered places and peoples inhabiting these unknown dimensions. According to new theories, scientists now believe that there are microscopic dimensions, far below the range of our senses, and according to String Theory (which suggests that subatomic particles are one-dimensional loops) there are at least ten dimensions of space. Our knowledge of dimensions is slowly increasing, and one day we may know enough to explain the following strange story, which was related to me several years ago.

In November 1975, Graham Edwards, a fifty-five-year-old widower, opened the pages of the *Liverpool Echo* and began to leaf through the pages until he came to the 'Houses for Sale' section. Amidst the columns of houses on offer, one particular house caught his eye:

NOCTORUM, Superior Semi-Detached; through
lounge with feature fireplace, fitted kitten, 3 bedrooms, bathroom, separate w.c.; central heating;
detached garage, large gardens with greenhouse
and fruit trees etc; for quick sale £8,000.
051-677 xxxx.

Graham was living in Liverpool with his ten-year-old son Marty, and since the tragic loss of his young wife Susannah to cancer, he had loathed the rented house in which they lived, because of all the terrible memories it held for him. He felt the same hatred towards Liverpool city centre, with all its shops and restaurants; all the places where he once went with Susannah. He decided it was time to make a new start and move to Wirral, and as he had a friend living in Oxton, Graham immediately telephoned the owner of the semi in Noctorum, in the hope of viewing the property.

He took Marty with him on the day of the viewing, and as the Ford Escort jockeyed for position in the lanes leading to the Queensway Tunnel, the boy asked his father if he would have to go to another school if they moved to the new house. "Probably, yes," Graham admitted honestly, and Marty said little for the remainder of the journey.

The house surpassed all Graham's expectations, although it was a little older than he had imagined, dating back to the 1920s. Nevertheless, it afforded a fine view of the local golf course and was set in a quiet neighbourhood. Within a week, Graham and his son had moved in, and arrangements were made for Marty to attend a local primary school that was just a five minute walk away.

Marty had a number of strange experiences sleeping in his new bedroom for the first time. He went to bed around 10pm, and awoke just after midnight to the aroma of frying bacon. He thought it was morning for a few moments, and that his father was making a special cooked breakfast for him, but the clock said it was two minutes past midnight. He bashed the pillow with his fist and then rested his head on it and returned to his slumbers, but at 1.30am he was awakened by faint voices. He sat up in bed, turned on the night-light, and listened. He could definitely hear voices in the distance, so he crept over to the window and carefully opened it.

The cold night air wafted in the delicate scent of autumn leaf-mould. He scanned the myrtle-coloured shades of the golf course and watched a night-mist crawl across the green. He could no longer hear the voices. Perhaps dad is watching the television, Marty thought, but soon after closing the window he heard his father's distinctive smoker's cough in the bedroom next door. That meant he had retired for the night, so the voices were not coming from the television.

The voices eventually faded away, but a week later, they returned. On this occasion, the eerie whispers awakened Marty at two in the morning, and soon after he opened his eyes, his nostrils were assailed with that same aroma of frying bacon. This time, Marty didn't sit up in bed, but listened all the same as he lay drowsily on his front with his head half-buried in the pillow. There were three people speaking, two male and one female. One voice was that of a young man, another that of a much older man, with a gravelly-sounding country accent. The other voice was a young woman's The harsh-voiced man was suddenly heard to shout, "Look yonder!"

"What is it?" asked the velvety female voice.

"Oi! You down there!" shouted the rough-sounding older voice.

That last sentence was much louder than the usual whispers in the darkness; in fact, it was so loud that it startled Marty, and he rolled over on to his back, looked straight up at the ceiling, and received the shock of his life. There were three people on his bedroom ceiling, or rather, the images of three people. A young woman in a strange lavender-pink, cone-shaped hat and matching attire, a young man of around fifteen dressed in a white shirt, dark leather jerkin and boots, and a balding, grey-bearded old man, incongruously dressed like the teenager. In the background there were fields, and in the centre of these fields was a quaint old fashioned village, partly obscured by the three outlandish figures. To the right of the three strangers, a pig was roasting on a spit over an open fire.

Marty did not immediately associate this spectacle with the aroma of bacon he had smelt on previous occasions. He froze as the bearded man knelt down near the ceiling rose and reached down to the flex of the light-fitting with a dirty hairy hand. It was as if he and the two others were kneeling on plate glass. The light shade swayed, and the woman in pink and the teenager gazed down at Marty with expressions of anxious fascination. Marty regained the ability to move, and threw his blankets clear, bolted from the bed and dashed to the bedroom door. In a moment he was in his father's room, violently shaking him awake. Graham Edwards awoke with a start, and in a furious voice shouted, "What the hell are you doing?"

Marty stammered out an incoherent account of the strange events that had unfolded on the ceiling of his bedroom, and his father stormed into the room to find nothing but the lightshade swinging like a pendulum. Marty hid behind him, scanning the ceiling for the three people he had seen earlier. Graham Edwards told his son he had simply had a nightmare, and ordered him to get back into bed. He was sure the whole episode had been some kind of attention seeking ploy to get him to change his mind about the move.

However, Marty did not sleep a wink all night, and kept gazing up at the ceiling, dreading the reappearance of the village scene, with its bizarre cast of characters. He was so tired on the following day from lack of sleep, that he dozed off twice in school. By the time it was bedtime again, he was hardly able to keep his eyes open.

At around 10pm he fell into a deep, dreamless sleep, and later awoke in the midst of a nightmare. He came to and found himself lying on cool grass, surrounding by people in strange outdated clothes. The woman in pink with the cone-shaped hat was bending over him, as was the old bald man with the grey beard. He was leaning over Marty, smiling to reveal missing front teeth. To Marty's right there stood a terrifying giant of a figure clad in grey metal armour.

As he bent down, a large red curly head with pointed swept-up eyebrows and penetrating dark eyes loomed towards him. Then something wet slobbered over his left hand, and he turned to see, of all things, a greyhound.

Marty crawled on his hands and knees away from the dog and the peculiar characters. He believed he was dreaming and crawled in a dream-like state to the edge of a circular hole, where he looked down to see his bedroom below. Then a jointed metal gauntlet with leather fingers landed with a painful thump on his right shoulder. Marty let out a high-pitched yelp and flung himself down the hole. He landed on the mattress of his bed, and bounced off after the impact and rolled across the floor.

When he looked up, he could see a circular aperture in the ceiling, as if he had been cast down into a pit. The weird people, and the greyhound, peered down at him, as he yanked open his bedroom door and once more ran in a state of utter terror to his dad's room. His father was enraged at being woken up at what turned out to be ten past four in the morning, but after seeing his son in tears, he hurried into his bedroom, and saw odd shadows moving across the ceiling. They slowly faded away, but Mr Edwards was deeply upset by the sight.

He set up his son's bedroom in another room and Marty enjoyed a good night's sleep from then on. The 'haunted room' – as Mr Edwards regarded it, was never slept in again, and it remained locked for years. On many occasions, in the wee small hours of the morning, he would hear strange voices and sounds emanating from that room. On one occasion he heard a girl's voice shouting "Dulcie!" but the meaning of that word (or name) has never been explained.

Graham Edwards spoke with a neighbour about the

haunted bedroom and was told that strange goings-on had been reported in the house since the 1930s. In 1981, Mr Edwards married a woman from Chester, and he and Marty gave up the house in Noctorum and went to live with her. The house is now inhabited, and as far as I know, there have been no ghostly intrusions in the bedroom, but these paranormal incidents have a habit of recurring when you least expect them, so we may not have heard the last about the mysterious village on the ceiling.

FORETOLD ON FRIDAY

There is an old and seemingly superstitious adage – that what you dream about on a Friday, and recount on a Saturday – will always come true. Here are just a couple of these weekend dreams that have been told to me by readers over the years.

In the late 1940s, a young woman named Patricia met a man a few years older than herself in the Melody Milk Bar on Liscard Road. His name was Henry, and although he lived down by Raby, he travelled to Liscard to see Patricia every other day. The couple became engaged a year after that first meeting, and Patricia started to plan the white wedding with her older sister Nancy.

One Friday night, Patricia went to bed, and endured a terrible nightmare, which she recalled on the Saturday. She told her mother how she had dreamt she was walking down the aisle on her father's arm, when she became aware that, on the altar, a coffin stood upright. The lid creaked open and there lay her husband-to-be, only he was wearing a priest's clothes and had pallid white skin and red hair. She had then awakened in a cold sweat.

Patricia's grandmother happened to overhear the description of the dream and in a sombre voice she told her that it would be sure to come true, because she had had the dream on a Friday and was recounting it on a Saturday. This obviously upset her and her mother told her grandmother off for being so superstitious.

Henry was supposed to visit her that weekend, but he failed to turn up. For three days Patricia did not hear a word from her future husband, and imagined that all kinds of terrible things had happened to him. Strangely, Henry had never given Patricia a contact telephone number of any sort, and, unlike today, mobile phones were still a science-fiction writer's pipe-dream. Few people in working class homes even had a land-line, so for three days, Patricia imagined the worst because of her grim dream.

Then, late on Tuesday night, Henry turned up at Patricia's home in Liscard with some bad news; his older brother Phillip had died in his sleep. It was thought that his weak heart had finally packed in. Just before the funeral, Henry showed Patricia a black and white photograph of his brother – and he was not only dressed as a priest, but bore an uncanny resemblance to Henry.

"He might look like me in black and white," Henry mused, surveying the photograph despondently, "but he had red hair."

All Patricia could manage, by way of reply, was an almost inaudible "Oh!" and she immediately recalled that the priest in the coffin in her dream had been red-haired. Henry then fought to keep back his tears, as he told Patricia how he had secretly arranged for his brother to officiate at their wedding. Before this, Henry had never mentioned that his brother was a man of the cloth, yet Patricia's dream had been a clear vision of Phillip's impending death. Her grandmother, hearing all this, chilled the girl by saying, "Didn't I tell you, pet? If you dream it on the Friday and recount it on the Saturday, it always comes true."

* * * *

In 1994, Rosie and Chris, a couple who had been seeing each other for five years, were sitting on a bench in Birkenhead Park, deep in conversation. Even a casual observer could not have failed to have noticed the agonised looks on both their faces, and it would not have come as a great surprise to learn that they had just decided to end their relationship. Both were married, and after much soul-searching, Rosie had declared that she could no longer go on being unfaithful, for she loved her husband as much as she loved Chris. She was also determined to ensure that her two young children would have some stability in their lives, instead of the broken home that would come with a divorce.

Chris could hardly speak for a while, because he knew that, for him, there would be nothing worth living for, once Rosie had left him. He took a ring out of his jacket pocket, a simple thin gold band – his late mother's wedding ring – the ring he had hoped to put on Rosie's finger one day, and he asked her to wear it. "You could say you found it amongst your old jewellery, or something … that it was a ring you'd bought for yourself years ago," Chris suggested, his eyes brimming with tears. "Please wear it to remember me …" His voice trailed off as they clung to each other – for the last time. His last words to Rosie were, "You know I'll love you till the day I die."

When Rosie reached home that night, her husband saw her red eyes and naturally asked why she was upset. She had to pretend that she had seen a dog knocked down by a car on her way home from work. He accepted her explanation without question, never suspecting a thing, as he had complete trust in her.

Life was almost unbearable without Chris, but Rosie was determined not to weaken and she would look at her children every time she felt the urge to telephone her ex-lover, and imagine the consequences for them, should she go back on her word. All the same, she always wore the ring he had given her to remember him by – as if she could ever forget him!

A year later, Rosie had a strange dream about Chris one night. He had often featured in her dreams since their split, but this was different. It started with an image of the Statue of Liberty of all things, then the next thing she knew, she was back in Birkenhead Park, and she was holding Chris's hand as she walked along – but he was dressed all in a white. Not only that, his suit was pearlescent, as were his shirt and shoes. She asked him why he was dressed in that way, and he said he was ready to go "over there". Rosie asked him where over there was, and with a slight smile he told her he was going into the "next life". Rosie became upset and said she wanted him to stay with her. The scene then changed dramatically. She was looking at a hospital ward, and there was Chris, lying in one of the beds, wired up to a monitor of some sort which was bleeping at his bedside.

When Rosie woke up she could not get the dream out of her mind and knew that it was no ordinary dream. What's more, she had had this dream on a Friday night, and recalled it on the Saturday. She told it in confidence to her best friend, Hannah, who was sure the dream was going to be prophetic. She recited the saying, "Dream it on a Friday, recall it on a Saturday, then it's sure to come true."

"Oh, thanks a lot for cheering me up, Hannah," said Rosie, trying to make light of her friend's insensitivity, but deep down she was really worried.

A few days later, to take her mind off Hannah's morbid claim, she took her two children to play in Birkenhead Park. They passed the very tree under which she and Chris had been standing on the day they had split up a year ago, and the painful emotions of that day almost overwhelmed her. She pondered the age of the towering tree, whose trunk was the size of a small room and wondered if it would still be there when she was dead and gone. She also realised that the eternal problem of being in love with two people at the same time would still be unacceptable, long after she had turned to dust.

Her mournful reveries came to an abrupt end when the ring that Chris had given her suddenly snapped on her finger. She actually felt it break apart, and her two children heard it too and looked at their mother's hand. Rosie knew in an instant that something had happened to Chris. She sensed a gaping cold void opening up, which could never be filled – even by the love of her wonderful children. This powerful sensation of sudden emptiness numbed her to the core. For her, the world would never be the same again.

A few weeks later, Ian, a man who had been a casual friend of Chris's, bumped into Rosie when she was out shopping in Liverpool. He told her that Chris had died a fortnight ago, whilst in New York, after suffering a massive heart attack. He had survived the initial attack, but died three days later in a hospital bed, without ever regaining consciousness. Ian had heard the sad news from Chris's sister and knowing about the affair, thought it right to pass it on. When Rosie asked for the exact date of his death, she realised that it was the same day on which her ring had snapped in the park.

Rosie went alone to Birkenhead Park the day after hearing this dreadful news. Beneath the old tree, she recalled Chris's last words to her, "You know I'll love you till the day I die". It seemed as if he had been true to his word. On the day he had died, the ring on Rosie's finger had snapped, perhaps symbolising the broken bond of something so rare in this troubled world today – true love.

DOUGHNUT HEAD

At a certain flat on Pensby Road, a strange apparition has been sighted for over forty years. The first recorded resident to see it was thirty-nine-year-old Sheila Taylor, on the appropriate date of Friday, 13 February 1970. Sheila was separated from her husband in Thingwall and had seen the flat advertised in a newsagent's window. The rent was five pounds a week, and was located within a few hundred yards of her mother's home. It seemed perfect and Sheila was keen to rent the flat.

However, after she had lived in the ground floor flat for five months, she began to suspect that she was not the only resident. On that fateful Friday the thirteenth, Sheila was sitting snuggled up with her gas fire on full, to ward off the February chill, glued to her little black and white television set. At 9.30pm, she was engrossed in an episode of the *Forsyte Saga* when she heard a massive bang, which left a ringing sound in her ears, and for a few seconds that was all she could hear. When it subsided, she went in search of the source of the explosion. She found nothing, and called on a next-door neighbour, thinking the bang may have originated in her flat, but it hadn't, and curiously, no one outside Sheila's flat had heard the loud blast.

A week later, again on a Friday, another loud bang almost deafened Sheila, this time about two hours later than the previous one. Once again, she searched her flat, trying to find the cause of the loud bang, but once more, she found nothing to explain it. On this occasion, Sheila was almost certain that the noise seemed to originate from her bedroom, but she saw nothing amiss in there.

On the following Friday, Sheila invited Cathy, an old schoolfriend from Egremont, over to the flat. Sheila had briefed her about the baffling bangs and her friend had argued that there had to be a rational explanation. That night, something would take place that would not only change her mind, but also send the two women fleeing the Pensby Road flat as if it were on fire.

At 11.40pm, Cathy came out of the toilet to be startled by a shadowy figure gliding past her in the unlit hallway, as if on castors. It was heading noiselessly for Sheila's bedroom and Cathy, sensing that she was looking at a ghost, cried out to her friend. Within seconds, Sheila dashed into the hallway, and Cathy was just telling her about the soundless intruder, when there was a deafening bang, followed by a dull thump, both plainly coming from the bedroom.

On tiptoe, Sheila inched towards her bedroom door and at the last second shoved it open. The room was in blackness, but she could smell something unfamiliar. She reached out and flicked the light-switch. Her index finger felt something wet on the switch. The light on, she saw that the yellow wallpaper was spattered with blood – as were the ceiling, carpet and furniture.

Cathy saw it first – the body of a man lying sprawled across the floor, with his head spread to three times its normal size and a huge hole in the middle through which the bloodied carpet was showing. The head reminded

Sheila of a ring doughnut and she shuddered at the ludicrous connection. Lying next to the man was a double-barrelled shotgun with a wisp of smoke drifting from its two barrels. For some obscure reason, one of the man's feet was bare, whilst on the other he wore a brown brogue-type shoe. Slivers of bone and brain tissue were sliding down the wardrobe mirror in rivulets of blood. An open eye was still attached to the torus of deformed flesh, blood, muscle and bone, and it jerked frantically in its torn-out socket, as though trying to glean information about its dire situation, but its fruitless searchings were more likely because of electrical activity in the cadaver's nervous system.

The two women staggered away from the grisly scene and Sheila promptly vomited on the floor and all over Cathy's slippers. Their first instinct was to get outside into the fresh air and they stood on the doorstep gasping in great lungsful of the stuff, as if to obliterate the horrific images which were searing into their brains. Neither girl had been able to utter a word, when suddenly they heard a noise behind them. They both shot round. Standing there, stock still in the bedroom doorway, was the man who had just taken his own life with a shotgun blast to the head.

In nightgown and slippers, Cathy ran off down the road, abandoning her friend. Fear affects people in different ways, and in Sheila's case, her legs seemed to lose all power and she couldn't run, which is what she desperately wanted to do. In fact, she could barely walk, but walk away she did without looking back, but after she had gone a few yards she heard the front door slam.

Although the bedroom later showed no trace of the sickening bloodbath that the girls had both witnessed, Sheila had no desire to return to that flat on Pensby Road.

Many other people have written to me and to other

researchers of the paranormal over the years, with descriptions of the apparition at the Pensby Road flat. I did a little research into this ghost and could find no printed reports connected to it in the newspaper archives. I therefore appealed to the public for information via the *Billy Butler Show*, on Radio Merseyside, being careful not to tell them what the ghost looked like. Nor did I make any mention of the shotgun, and yet within a few minutes of making the on-air appeal, Alec Young, who took the callers' phone numbers, was inundated with statements from listeners. They rang in from places as far apart as Mold and Manchester, each with their own account of the hauntings on Pensby Road.

One man, Wilf Jones, told how his flat on Pensby Road had a ghost that turned on the taps and switched on the kettle in the early hours, and on one occasion, shook him awake at four o'clock in the morning. This apparition was of a man, around six foot three inches height, but Wilf didn't live at the address haunted by 'doughnut head' so I presumed he was talking about another ghost.

I telephoned about a dozen other people who had supernatural tales to tell about Pensby Road, but none of them mentioned the address that I was interested in. Then I struck lucky, because a retired nurse named Karen was the next on the list, and not only did she identify the flat in question, but also told me that she too had seen the gory-looking phantom. This was in 1978 when she lived in that same flat on Pensby Road.

Like Sheila and Cathy, Karen heard the bangs, which, presumably, were some sort of ghostly re-enactment of the suicide (or possibly an accident). At first, Karen had tried to rationalise the peace-shattering sounds by putting forward innocent explanations. The first bang was thought to be a car back-firing, and the next to be a blown fuse – even though no electrical item in the flat had short-circuited. The third bang took place in late February 1978; Karen was unsure of the exact date. It is interesting to note that the bangs Sheila and Cathy had heard in the flat eight years before this, were also in February.

Then one morning, at around 1.30am, in late February 1978, Karen got up to go the toilet in the middle of the night, when she heard the third bang. She stepped into the hall and in the semi-darkness saw a man standing there in a light-coloured shirt. The collar and right shoulder of the shirt were heavily stained in blood, and the head was a drooping loop of hair, flesh and blood. Karen's screams would have wakened the dead and the grotesque figure vanished. She got dressed as quickly as she could and abandoned the flat, only to return just once more with her brother to collect her belongings. She told me that there was an atmosphere of hate there that was almost palpable.

"I once walked into a room after a couple had had a blazing row and I could feel the atmosphere of hate still hanging in the air," she told me, "and every few days whilst I was living in the flat I felt those same type of vibes in that bedroom. It was like an after-image of some argument ... or as if someone was really detested there once."

Karen believes she has inherited mediumistic talents from her mother, and when I tried to talk her into revisiting the haunted flat, "No way!" was her unequivocal answer.

A woman named Ruth also emailed me and asked if I thought the ghost might be that of a man who had committed suicide on Pensby Road in the 1930s. She told me that she had heard about a tragic suicide at a house on the road that was later converted into flats. According to the account Ruth had learned from her late father, a man had repeatedly sent love letters to a woman who didn't return his affection, and in the end he warned her that he would end his life if he couldn't have her as his wife. What's more, his blood would be on her hands for the rest of her life.

The woman, who was a well-known beauty in the neighbourhood, laughingly dismissed his threat and said "You may go and jump in the river, for all I care!" and that evening she instructed her boyfriend to deliberately drive his convertible car, with her in it, past the house of her demented admirer on their way to a party in Birkenhead. Her cruel stunt did not go unnoticed and moments after the car had passed the house of her lovesick admirer, he took off a shoe and sock, placed the shotgun barrels in his mouth, and pulled the trigger with his big toe. This latter piece of information neatly explained why the body that Sheila and Kathy saw lying on the bedroom floor had one bare foot, devoid of sock and shoe ...

However, just whose ghost is haunting the flat on Pensby Road still remains a mystery, as Ruth was unable to supply me with a name. Perhaps someone reading these words knows the truth, or may hold that little piece of vital information that could explain the whys and wherefores behind the haunting. If you do know anything, and wish to share it with me, please contact me via my publishers at the address given at the end of this book.

THE MOGGAN-TAR

On a bitterly cold day in the late winter of 1980, fifty-nine-year-old Stephen was sweeping the search coil of his metal detector across the snow-covered grass of Thurstaston Common, (situated almost two miles north west of Heswall). He was looking for his lost wedding ring, which he thought must have slid off whilst he was walking across the common. The raw cold had chilled him to the bone and he was just about to give up the search, when he made an intriguing discovery – but more of that in a moment.

Today, Thurstaston Common has been designated as an SSSI – a Site of Special Scientific Interest – but in 1980 it was mostly regarded as a welcome green space, a wild place in which to wander and take refuge from the rat race. The common is the best example in the UK of a lowland heathland, and its name is thought to be derived from either Thorstein's Farm, or – more romantically – Thor's stone. In support of the latter theory, there is on the common a massive rectangular-shaped block of sandstone, thirty feet in width and fifty feet in length, which is known as 'Thor's Stone'. Sadly, the rock's surface has been defaced with carved-out graffiti, but despite this vandalism, which dates back over a century, Thor's Stone still retains a mysterious quality, which fits well with its supernatural history.

In the first place, there was once a 'Faery Well' quite close to the stone, of which all traces now seem to have vanished. I mentioned this lost well on the radio once and many elderly people in Wirral, Liverpool and North Wales telephoned me on air to say that they had taken flowers to the Faery Well as children. In the second place, a belief has existed for many years that the unusual ruddiness of Thor's

Stone is not due solely to the fact that it is made of sandstone, but to a far more sinister reason. According to this theory, its rusty colouration has been caused by all the blood sacrifices that have taken place there in secret over the years. Some say the Danes used the stone as a sacrificial altar to some long-forgotten God – or perhaps even to Thor himself. There are also local rumours that sacrifices were carried out on the rock as late as the 1930s.

Now back to 1980. In the Arctic March of that year, snowstorms blanketed the UK and 70mph gale-force winds lashed the country, uprooting trees, swiping slates of rooftops and bringing down power-lines. Vehicles travelling along the M62 Pennine route between Rochdale and Oldham were blown over and the eastbound carriageway was blocked for hours by the continuous heavy snowfall, which was whipped up by the wind into gigantic meringues, with swirls and peaks up to five feet high.

Whilst most people with any common sense were sheltering indoors, our middle-aged hero, Stephen, originally a shopkeeper from Crosby but now living in retirement near Irby Heath, was still battling out the storm on Thurstaston Common. The tone of his metal detector had suddenly changed to the steady high pitched whine that indicated that he had found metal. Could it be his precious wedding ring? He took out his spade, and after scraping away a thick layer of the pristine snow, he began digging into the tough frozen soil of the common, close to Thor's Stone. The work was difficult and he could only chip away tiny fragments at a time, but the exertion had banished the creeping numbness from his limbs.

After about ten minutes, the spade hit the edge of something metallic. It was a large rusted sphere with two holes in it, and from these holes there ran wires which bound a small crucifix to its back. Stephen prised the sphere from the ground and hurled it to one side. He had temporarily forgotten all about the reason for his search, and just wanted to know what lay beneath the circular patch of dark soil on which the metal lid had rested. He had to know. He grabbed his metal detector and his excitement rose as the orange meter-needle indicated that something lay buried there.

For almost half a minute, the setting sun shone feebly beneath the low oppressive snow clouds, as it abandoned the sky, dragging the grey day below the mist-blurred horizon. Stephen's spade glanced off something in the dark soil, and he cursed himself for being so careless. He took off a glove, and with his naked hand he reached into the hole that lay beneath. His fingers gently wiped away the cold moist soil to reveal a large, almost circular lump. He plunged his other gloved hand into the hole and slowly and carefully began to excavate the soil and clay from the intriguing find. By touch alone, he soon realised that what he was holding was a head – a head with the ears of a cat.

Not long afterwards, as the snow started to come down heavily once again, and the wind sent it slicing into Stephen's face, so that he could scarcely breathe, he extracted a heavy artefact from the hole in the ground and studied it in the gathering gloom. It was an evil-looking effigy of a large cat, fashioned from a lead-like metal. It measured about thirty inches in height and around ten to twelve inches in diameter and weighed around twenty-two pounds.

What with the atrocious weather, the weight of the object and Stephen's poor physical condition, he had quite a job carrying the feline figure back to his cottage, but he was totally captivated by his find and was determined to get a good look at it indoors.

That evening, after he had warmed up and dried out in front of the fire, he laid the object out on a piece of newspaper and set about cleaning it. Once the dirt had been removed, he proudly stood the cat on his kitchen table, then washed and dried his hands, lit a cheroot, and sat and surveyed the peculiar effigy. He was very pleased with the cat, which, with its penetrating eyes, furrowed brow and fierce fanged mouth, would make an excellent guardian on the hearthstone of his fireplace. He placed it a little distance from the fire, as the cat was seemingly clad in a metal that looked and felt like a hard lead alloy.

The retired shopkeeper sat with a glass of West Indian Madeira wine, wondering how old the cat was and who had made it and buried it in such an isolated place. Only then did he remember his lost wedding ring, which had slipped off his thinning finger somewhere on the common weeks before. Never in his wildest dreams did he imagine finding something like this. He knew he was supposed to declare it to the authorities, but he was already falling in love with this weird cat, and decided he could not bear to part with it.

Instead, Stephen resolved to visit his good friend Peter in the morning. He was a man with a vast knowledge of archaeology and folklore, as well as being a fount of blood-curdling ghost stories. Halfway through the bottle of Madeira, Stephen dozed off in front of the blazing fire, as the snow-laden wind whistled down the chimney and rattled the cottage windows. At around eleven o'clock that evening, Stephen woke up in his winged, William and Mary-styled fireside armchair. For one heart-stopping moment he thought he saw the cat from Thurstaston Common looking around his room. He rubbed his bleary eyes and looked again. No, the cat was as still as a stone and in exactly the same place he had put it.

On the following morning, shortly before eleven, Peter called at the cottage, and the moment he set eyes on the cat, the welcoming smile he was accustomed to wearing when visiting his friend quickly evaporated. "What's that?" he asked, seconds after his arrival. He knelt by the hearth, the better to examine it, but seemed reluctant to touch the mystifying figure.

Stephen laughed as he told him how he had gone out on his obsessive quest to find his lost wedding ring in the snowstorm, and had found 'Felix' instead.

"On the common?" asked Peter, backing away from the hearth.

"Yes," said Stephen. "How did you know?"

"Near to the altar stone?" said Peter, now resting his hand on the mantelpiece, his face ashen.

"*What* stone?" asked Stephen, not understanding what he was talking about.

"You know, Thor's Stone!" Peter shouted, with mounting impatience; a reaction that was entirely out of character for a man known for his impeccable manners and who was always softly spoken.

Jarred by the tone and volume of his friend's reply, Stephen replied, in a meek voice, "Yes, that stone ... why?"

Peter had now moved further away from the cat, and was perched on the edge of a two-seater sofa at the back of the room, with his gaze fixed upon the unearthed artefact. He looked his friend in the eye and in a grave voice, recalled the old stories his father had told him. "Have you ever heard of the Moggan-Tar?" he asked.

Stephen shook his head, "No."

At last, Peter averted his gaze from the cat and spoke directly to Stephen. "Well, there used to be ... well there probably still is ... a society of, well, pagans ... if that's the word. They used to kill people up on that stone altar ... on Thor's Stone."

"Kill people? You're kidding!"

"Yes, they killed people alright. They were held down while they had their throats cut; sacrificed to some idol the pagans believed in as much as we believe in the Almighty."

"Oh come on, Peter, the authorities would have been on to them if they went round sacrificing people," Stephen said and gave a nervous laugh, knowing deep down that he didn't want to believe in this ghastly pagan business.

"Hundreds of people still go missing every year," Peter replied, glancing back at the cat, "and many of them are never seen or heard from again. Believe me, I've researched this demonic idol ... it's known by the ancient nickname of Moggan-Tar, but the precise etymology of the name eludes me. Perhaps there's some tenuous link with the quaint old term, 'moggie' and Moggan, or the answer could lie in the Manx language ... on the Isle of Man there's the Moddey Doo, the black devil dog of Peel Castle."

Stephen cleared out the ashes of the fire as Peter recounted a story of his mythical demon cat.

"I've researched as far back as eighteen seventy-eight. That year, John Pugsley, a gamekeeper at Thurstaston Hall, saw a huge black cat with glowing eyes whilst out on the common. He shot at it from close range but the creature sloped away unharmed. That same year, gypsies camped on the common also saw the animal and believed it to be a supernatural entity associated with a healing well."

"I wonder if that's the so-called Faery Well that was supposed to exist near to Thor's Stone?" said Stephen, as he shovelled ashes from the grate on to some spread out newspaper pages.

Peter gave his friend's question some thought for a

couple of moments, then shrugged and continued relating the catalogue of strange incidents from the annals of the fiendish feline.

"The same Devil Cat, as the locals called it, was seen in the summer of eighteen ninety-five, in broad daylight, when it attacked two sheep dogs on the common. It even appeared during the sheep dog trials and tried to drag off a sheep after tearing its throat out. It was blasted at point blank range by a shotgun, and the shot bounced off it as if it were made of metal."

"Steady on a bit, Peter. That's rather far-fetched, if you don't mind me saying so, even by your storytelling standards," Stephen remarked flippantly, and parcelled up the ashes with a grin.

"Then it's no use me going on any further," said Peter sulkily, turning away.

"Oh, I'm sorry," said Stephen, trying to sound sincere. "Please go on. I was enjoying it."

But Peter was offended by his friend's cynical attitude and couldn't be persuaded to continue his history of the Moggan-Tar, until Stephen had built a new fire and it was roaring in the grate. Even then he demanded whiskey because, he maintained, he had a sore throat coming on.

Feeling a little more relaxed with a glass of whiskey in his hand, Peter told Stephen how the locals, believing that the Moggan-Tar was the Devil in disguise, would leave meat out for him near the well. Sometimes local families would forsake their Sunday roast and take a whole joint of beef instead to Thor's Stone. Those who left meat for the cat in this way seemed to prosper. And so it was that, somewhere along the way, a child was offered in place of the meat, in the hope of gaining greater luck and success.

In the 1930s, two Irish priests bravely decided to tackle

the Moggan-Tar and consecrated the ground around the well from where it was said to emerge. The cat was driven into the depths of the ancient well by the bell, book and candle rite, and a lid with a crucifix attached was afterwards placed over the well's mouth.

A faint cold sweat broke out on Stephen's forehead as he recalled the rusted lid and crucifix.

"The right thing to do is to put it back," Peter advised, and he sipped the whisky and grimaced at the cat on the hearth.

"Not likely! We should get it valued – bet it's worth a bob or two."

As Peter was explaining why the figure should be returned to the place where it had been unearthed, Stephen went to a cupboard, pulled open a draw, and took out a case containing his camera. He wound a lever, pulled back the curtains to admit the diffused daylight from the bright snowscape outside and took two photographs of the Moggan-Tar.

Peter was disgusted by his friend's talk of money and his plan to sell the sinister figure to the highest bidder. An argument ensued and Peter stormed out after throwing the dregs from his glass of whiskey into the fire.

Later that day, Gloria, Stephen's sister-in-law, called on him to see how he was. She was the younger sister of his late wife, Joan. Gloria – or 'Glo' as Stephen called her, immediately noticed the Moggan-Tar sitting on the hearth. She remarked on it but her brother-in-law did not mention a word about the supernatural history of the idol. Later, in the evening, something took place which almost gave Stephen a heart attack and made Gloria feel faint. She was sitting in the fireside armchair, leafing through old photographs of her deceased sister, when she suddenly yawned, rubbed her eyes, and relaxed back into the chair. Stephen went to fetch a bottle of wine from the kitchen, and as Gloria waited for her glass to be poured, she idly stroked the head of the Moggan-Tar, which was now silhouetted against the lively flames of the coal fire. Stephen was in the kitchen, uncorking a bottle of wine, when he heard her scream. He almost dropped the bottle as he ran into the living room.

"It ... it bit me!" Gloria gasped, standing on the hearth rug, gazing down at the statue of the cat as she rubbed her right hand. "That horrible thing bit me!"

She staggered past Stephen's outstretched arms towards the kitchen in shock. She told him how the cat's head had turned to bite her hand as she was stroking it.

Stephen noticed the trickle of blood on the little finger of her right hand and was just about to wash it and put a plaster on it, when Gloria let out another scream. The cat had suddenly sprung to life. It turned its face towards Stephen and he saw that its eyes were now burning red. The thing hissed like an angry snake, and showed its deadly-looking metal fangs.

Stephen grabbed the bottle of wine and flung it at the accursed thing but to no effect; it bounced off the creature's dull metallic back and smashed against the stone fire surround. The Moggan-Tar leaped into the fire and scrambled about for a moment amongst the flames, kicking lumps of red hot coals out of the grate with its back legs. Then it jumped up the chimney with true cat-like agility, sending showers of soot and sparks showering down on to the fireplace and hearth.

Gloria and Stephen clung to one another, speechless with disbelief, as they listened to the eldritch scuttling down the snow-covered slates of the roof, and it was visible for a brief instant through one of the cottage windows, as it leapt to the ground. Stephen clutched his chest. He felt sick and weak. Gloria too felt faint with fear, but was somehow able to comfort him and calm him down. They both sat on the sofa, clutching each other and gazing in silence into the fire for a very long time.

All Stephen had left were the two photographs he had taken of the malevolent cat. The whole episode had left him feeling very wobbly, and whether it was the cold up on the common, or the way the cat had come to life, he went to his doctor complaining of chest pains, and told him exactly what had happened. The doctor responded with an apparent non sequiter, asking if there was adequate ventilation at the cottage, because a build up of carbon monoxide was known to cause all kinds of hallucinations.

Few people were prepared to believe Stephen's whacky story – but Peter and Gloria knew better.

Some believe that the occasional reports of a big cat on Thurstaston Common are actually sightings of the evil Moggan-Tar. As recently as August 2007, a group of teenagers riding mountain bikes near Thor's Stone, reported seeing the black silhouette of a huge cat draped atop the sandstone landmark. The creature had the telltale red glowing eyes, and was surrounded by a colourful aura. It also looked ready to pounce, so the young bikers didn't stick around and rode off as fast as they could.

QUIRKUS

There is a house on Noctorum's Beryl Road that was the scene of some very strange goings-on in the early 1970s. The dwelling was a detached, four-bedroom house with a well-kept front garden which was arrayed with a spectrum of beautiful summer flowers and a large rear garden where the children often played.

In early October 1972, ten-year-old Hardy Jones lived at this house with his thirteen-year-old sister Suzanne. One Saturday afternoon, their parents went to Birkenhead to buy birthday presents for Suzanne and left her in charge of the house and also asked her to keep an eye on Hardy. Although it was October, it was a sunny afternoon, and Suzanne was sitting on a deck chair in the back garden, with a sketchbook on her knee, drawing with coloured felt-tip pens. She was not sketching from real life, but from her imagination, which often throws up the most unexpected images. In this way she created a tall man with long black curly hair and a turned-up, tapering thin moustache, of the type associated with the surrealist artist, Salvador Dali.

Hardy dribbled his football over to her deck chair and glanced at the sketch. "Who's that?" he asked, angling his head sideways.

"Mm, I don't know," Suzanne replied dreamily, as she gave her creation a long white gown and a golden cape.

"What's that silly dress he's wearing?" Hardy queried with a grin. "Looks like gran's nightie."

"Oh, go away, will you, you little pest? You're annoying me," Suzanne said, and her brother kicked the ball into a far corner of the garden, and then ran off to retrieve it.

On the grass, about two feet away from the deck chair, a

transistor radio that Suzanne had been listening to earlier, suddenly switched itself on at full volume. The tune that blared out from the radio made the spooky incident twice as disturbing. It was a song from the charts by Jamaican singer-songwriter Dandy Livingstone, entitled 'Suzanne Beware of the Devil' – and the effect it had on Suzanne Jones was immediate. She almost fell out of the deck chair as she lunged sideways to switch off the radio.

Hardy stood like a statue watching his sister on her knees, clicking off the radio.

"Did you see that then?" she asked him.

"Yeah! How did it happen? You didn't touch it, did you?"

"No, I didn't and I've no idea how it happened," Suzanne told him, as a long cloud slid across the sun, instantly changing the atmosphere in the garden. A wind stirred and Suzanne felt goose-bumps rising on her arms. She looked back at her sketchpad. The man was now smiling. She had not drawn his face that way, and she knew that her brother had not been anywhere near it.

The sudden sombre mood was broken by the sound of the icecream van on Beryl Road; the beautiful lilting melody of Greensleeves corrupted into an irritating jangle. However, what was noise pollution and an unwelcome intrusion to the adults in leafy Beryl Road, was music to their children's ears and brought them running out of their houses as if the Pied Piper were calling them. Suzanne was faced with a bit of a dilemma; she had enough pocket money to buy herself a cornet, but what about Hardy? "I wish I had another five pence," she mumbled to herself, and went into the kitchen in search of one.

On the gingham tablecloth covering the kitchen table she noticed a dark coin-shaped object. She reached out and picked it up and found that it was indeed a fivepenny piece, although, for some reason, the coin felt warm and was unusually dark in colour. Suzanne did not ponder the mystery long, for there were far more pressing matters at hand – like ice cream!

She ran out of the front door, bought the two ice creams and handed one to Hardy, who had run out after her. Mission accomplished, she gave no more thought to the blackened five pence piece, which had looked as if it had been burned, and went back into the garden. She stopped short when she reached the patio, for the radio had been switched on again.

Suzanne's heart began to pound inside her chest and she looked round nervously, as Hardy licked the raspberry sauce from his fingers, seemingly oblivious. A faint voice started whispering in her ear, but she couldn't make out what it was saying. Just then, a bumble bee started buzzing round her, attracted by the smell of the raspberry sauce. She tried to shoo it away and in doing so, the hand holding the cornet tilted violently and the blob of ice cream fell out. It landed on Suzanne's shoe and began to ooze down the sides. She swore in frustration and kicked off her shoe, and the melting ice cream flew into a bush.

"Ooh! I'm telling mum you swore!" said Hardy, making exaggerated licking noises as he devoured his ice cream. "Mm, this ice cream's delicious!"

"You ungrateful little brat," said Susan. "That's the last time I buy you anything."

"Only kidding," said Hardy. "Can't you take a joke?"

Suzanne then went inside to wipe her shoe with a towel, and as she was coming out again she suddenly noticed Hardy – he was holding his ice cream about a foot away from his mouth without eating it. At the same time, he was gazing with wide eyes and an open mouth at something in the dark corner of the garden. Suzanne followed his gaze and saw a tall man standing by some shrubs. He looked exactly like the figure she had drawn earlier in her sketchbook. He had long black curly hair, that same outlandish elongated twisted up moustache and was wearing a long white garment reminiscent of the white cassock worn by priests during services. Over the weird stranger's shoulders there hung a stunning cape, lined with silken gold, which reached down to his waist.

"Hey!" the figure shouted, and took one step towards them, revealing his footwear, which was outlandishly long and pointed.

Suzanne grabbed Hardy by the shoulders and dragged him into the house. She closed the kitchen door, but didn't have the strength her father possessed to slide the bolt into the receiver on the door frame. Meanwhile, the figure was steadily approaching, so the children ran in mute terror into the hallway. That kitchen door never opened, and yet, behind them, Hardy and Suzanne could hear the rustle of their pursuer's garments and the faint padding of his curled up footwear inside the house.

As Suzanne opened the front door, she could see him out of the corner of her eye, coming out of the kitchen. She pushed Hardy out through the doorway and closed the door behind her, and as she heard the Yale latch click, she realised that she had effectively locked herself out. She and Hardy, who was now tearful, hurried down Beryl Road, and kept looking back, expecting what they now realised could only be a ghost, to be close behind – but so far he was nowhere to be seen.

Mr and Mrs Carson, a couple in their seventies, were walking towards Hardy and Suzanne, and they were the first to hear about the bizarre character who had chased them from their own garden and home. Mr Carson smirked, and then bent down and said to Hardy, who was holding the remnants of his melted ice cream, "Ghosts will never harm you, lad." He then winked at Suzanne, as if he thought Hardy had made the whole story up. Suzanne held Hardy's hand and hurried past them along the road. She decided to go to her schoolfriend's home in Shrewsbury Road. Angie Thomas was not in, but her mother, eyeing Hardy's red eyes and Suzanne's strained face, asked her what the matter was.

"This man chased us," Suzanne told her. "He came into the garden and then chased us."

"Come in, love. Come in, Hardy," said Mrs Thomas, ushering the two of them into the living room, where her husband was dozing under a newspaper in his armchair.

"Harry," said Mrs Thomas, tapping her husband's bald head and smiling at the children. He awoke with a start. When Suzanne told him what had happened, he looked at her and Hardy rather scathingly and advised them to go and tell their own parents.

"Their mum and dad are in Birkenhead shopping ... Suzanne's just told you that," Mrs Thomas chided him.

"Okay, I never heard that part, I'm still half asleep," he complained. "Be nice to get a bit of peace round here."

At that moment, a key rattled in the front door, and in came Angie Thomas, having just popped out to her friend's to borrow some records. Suzanne and Hardy went with her up into her bedroom, and as they climbed the stairs, Mr Thomas, still irritated by being woken up, shouted up to his daughter, "Don't you be going anywhere near that weird fellah. Got that?"

"Oh shurrup," Angie replied under her breath, and whispered to Suzanne that he was an "old narky knickers" as she showed them into her messy bedroom. As she had listened to Suzanne's story, Angie's eyes had grown wider and wider, and she tried to make some sense of the tale. She loved anything to do with the supernatural, and she began to theorise about what had happened. "You must be psychic," she said to Suzanne.

"Why? What makes you say that?"

"Well, you started drawing that fellah first, and then he appeared. You must have been tuning into him ... in a sort of psychic way."

Suzanne had never thought of it like that. "But who is he?" she wondered.

"I don't know," Angie shrugged, then her eyes widened even more and her dark eyebrows arched upwards. "Hey, maybe if you are psychic you can tune into the ghost somehow ... you know ... communicate with him," she suggested.

At this, Hardy's bottom lip protruded again and began to wobble. He was scared; terrified, in fact. Angie hugged him and said he had nothing to worry about.

"But I don't want to tune in," said Suzanne and glanced uneasily out of the window.

Angie rummaged through the mess on her dressing table and picked up an eyebrow pencil and then managed to locate her school homework book under a pile of half-worn clothes. She turned to a blank page and putting the pencil in Suzanne's hand, said, "Just sit there, and close your eyes and write the first thing that comes into your mind."

Suzanne was having none of it. She let out a profanity and angrily handed the pencil back. "No, I really don't want to. This isn't funny, you know. I just want to wait here till my mum and dad come back, that's all."

But somehow, the persistent Angie eventually managed to persuade Suzanne to carry out the psychic experiment.

Cream soda and some cakes were brought up and served to make the atmosphere less tense. Suzanne sat cross-legged on Angie's bed, eyebrow pencil in one hand, exercise book in the other. She pictured the scary figure in her garden, and recalled the sound of his voice as he shouted, "Hey!"

Her hand started scribbling and Angie snatched the book from her as soon as she had stopped writing. This time it was not a picture but a word, and it didn't look like Suzanne's writing. The word she had written was 'Quirkus'.

"And you didn't just make that up?" Angie asked, slightly suspicious.

"I swear I didn't. It just came out of nowhere, I didn't even think," Suzanne said, and she sounded completely sincere.

"You swear on your brother's life?" Angie asked with an intense look in her mascara ringed eyes.

"Yes, I swear on Hardy's life," Suzanne declared without a moment's hesitation, and her brother let out a gulp in the silence that followed.

"Wonder what it could mean?" Angie said, re-reading the scrawled word.

"Don't say it!" Suzanne suddenly shouted, not really knowing why. "Don't say it out loud!" Hardy jumped. The boy was now a jittering wreck.

"What's the matter?" asked Angie, startled by her friend's sudden outburst.

"I just have this really bad feeling, that even saying that name is asking for trouble."

"Quirkus? You mean just saying it?" said Angie, unable to stop herself.

"No! Don't even say his name, or he'll come here," Suzanne said, desperation creeping into her voice. Then she promptly jumped off the bed and told Hardy they were going home.

"But why are you leaving? Just because I said a stupid name ..." cried Angie, following after her friend as she opened the bedroom door. But seeing her determination to be off, she added at full volume, "Well that's it! You're not by best friend from now on!"

By the time Suzanne and Hardy had got back to Beryl Road, their parents were also back from Birkenhead. Their car was in the drive and the front door was wide open. The children were scolded for leaving the house, and neither parent believed the story about Quirkus and the black five pence piece, which, in any case, was not Suzanne's to take.

On the following evening, Suzanne was sitting in her room, thinking about Angie's harsh words, when she decided to do some drawing. She had always drawn, whether she was listening to music, talking, or watching the television; it was second nature to her. She picked up the big sketch book, and the first thing she saw was the picture of Quirkus and she tore it out and crumpled it in her hands. She threw the screwed up ball of paper into the waste basket and sat on her bed, gazing out at a thin crescent moon hanging over the silhouetted rooftops of the skyline.

A ruffling noise made her jump. It came from her yellow plastic waste bin. She looked in the bin and saw the crumpled-up sketch of the uncanny caped man unfurling itself like a time-lapse movie of a rosebud unfolding its petals. Her first instinct was to run out of the room, but this time she stayed put, although slowly backing away from the bin. Within seconds, the surreal figure from the garden the day before, was making his second appearance. This time, his head slid out from the gap behind the wardrobe – a ridiculously narrow gap of less than an inch, which separated the wardrobe from the wall.

As the entity was slithering out in this impossible

manner, Suzanne was overcome with weakness and collapsed on to her bed, where she began to hyperventilate with panic. However, in a strange accent, the entity urged her not to be afraid, he wasn't going to harm her.

"Get away from me," the girl gasped, and raised her trembling palm. Incongruous scents of linen and rosewater pervaded the room, and Suzanne began to experience déjà vécu – a very bizarre phenomenon, in which the person feels as if they have already lived through the moments they are currently going through. The phenomenon is often wrongly termed déjà vu – which literally means 'already seen' and applies to thinking you have *seen* something before, and only applies to sight. Déjà vécu applies to all of the senses, and the person experiencing it really believes that they have been in the exact position before, and so are able to predict exactly what someone will say and know what events are about to take place before they even happen.

In Suzanne's case, the sensation lasted for a couple of minutes, instead of persisting for the usual brief moment, and during that time she felt as if she knew the strange man standing before her as a close friend. Somehow she knew his name was Quirkus and that he had something to do with an ancient sorcerer named Simon Magus. She was very close to him, and yet it was all so long ago and in another place. He wasn't romantically connected to her in any way, but he had loved her all the same and she had loved him lifetimes ago, when her name had been Wreema. In her mind's eye Suzanne could envisage a vast desert, and she was looking out at this arid landscape from the entrance of a cool cave.

Then, just as suddenly as it had come upon her, the sensation went away and she was back in her bedroom. She heard her father calling her at the top of his voice from the bottom of the stairs. Then she heard his heavy footsteps on the landing outside her room. She looked up and saw tears in the eyes of the supernatural visitor.

"Say my name, or write my name, and I shall always come for you," the robed man whispered with pain evident in his voice and the lines etched on his forehead.

At this, he started to become transparent and Suzanne could see her bedroom door through him. As she was puzzling over this, the door burst open, and her father barged into the room. The quivering remnants of Quirkus' outline vanished, but the sweet scents of his linen and the rosewater lingered for a little while longer.

"What's the matter with you? Why don't you answer when I call you?" her father shouted, all red faced and panting from running up the stairs. He sniffed the air and asked what the sweet smell was. In those days, girls did not possess incense burners and scented candles, as many of them do now, and the pleasant fragrance was much richer and more pungent than any of Suzanne's or her mother's perfumes.

Suzanne had never heard about reincarnation at that age, but today she firmly believes that she has lived before, and that many of us have done the same, although we are not aware of it. She believes that when great friendships, or love affairs, end abruptly, because of a person's death, the soul often erases the painful memories, so the person will not become heartbroken from the loss in their next life – but some loves and friendships are so strong, that the soul's erasure mechanism does not always succeed in wiping all the memories away.

If reincarnation is true, it would mean that you could walk past a person in the street who may seem like a stranger, but he or she may have been your soul-mate in a previous state of existence.

Suzanne's partial recollection of a Simon Magus was particularly intriguing, because he was a powerful practitioner of the Occult in Samaria, and was mentioned in the New Testament (Acts 8 v.9-24). Simon the Sorcerer, as he came to be known, came to prominence just as orthodox religion was in decline and the peoples of the Mediterranean sought advice from mediums, astrologers and fake miracle workers. Simon was no fake, according to the Bible, and could fly and levitate. He was finally converted to Christianity by Philip the evangelist. Before his conversion, he had offered to pay large sums of money to the Apostles, if they would teach him the art of the laying on of hands to cure illnesses.

Unfortunately, in the end, Simon came to believe that he was himself a god, and levitated high above a crowd of would-be followers. Saint Peter, seeing this, prayed to God, asking him to stop Simon's ambition, upon which he suddenly plummeted to the ground, fracturing his legs in many places. He later died as two surgeons attempted to operate on him.

That a young girl from Noctorum should have established a connection with such a prominent figure from the Bible, presents us with a very great mystery.

FAKING IT

Many years ago, a witch who went by the name of Alice Raven, lived in rural Heswall. I am not sure if that was her real name, as I have never found her in any census, although there were many Romany folk like her who managed to evade the census over the years.

Alice settled in Wirral in the 1970s, after having roamed the land by caravan from the 1950s, with her sister Gormraith. The two women had lived in Norfolk for seven years, and then had moved on to Lincoln, where they settled for a year or so, but were moved on by a group of militant Christians, who suspected the sisters of practising malevolent witchcraft. And so they finally settled on Wirral, where, by and large, they minded their own business, although they were occasionally consulted by a trusted group of people who required help in the form of charms, potions and spells.

One fine summer's day, in the 1990s, Alice Raven travelled to a certain place in the North West to meet another witch. After they had enjoyed a cup of tea at a café, they noticed a small shop which sold what could be termed 'New Age paraphernalia'; things like crystals, athames, 'magical' herbs, crystal balls and various books on witchcraft. When Alice met the shop owner, she immediately sensed that he was a charlatan, even though he billed himself as a medium. Let us call this man Robert – not his real name. He offered a variety of services, including advising people about their future, reading their auras, and contacting relatives who had passed on.

Alice decided to put the fraudulent medium to the test, and started pitching questions at him that could only be answered correctly by one who was truly knowledgeable of the Occult. He tried to worm his way out of the questioning by hollow rhetoric and bluff, and several potential clients in the shop who overheard the bogus medium's replies were not at all impressed and instead of buying his potions and paraphernalia, or seeking his 'psychic advice', they chatted to Alice instead.

Robert was furious and ordered her and Gormraith off the premises. Alice cursed him on the spot. She warned him that the Fay (faery folk) and genuine spirits would exact their revenge on him for misrepresenting them. "He who pretends to speak on behalf of spirits will pay a dear price," she warned, as she stormed out of the shop followed by three or four disillusioned customers.

I have it on trusted authority that Robert had an incredible run of bad luck after that run-in with Alice Raven. He opened up his shop one morning to find the place wrecked, and initially believed he had been burgled, but a police investigation ruled this out. Instead, suspicion fell upon Robert himself, and there were claims that he had smashed up his shop as part of some insurance scam, although he vehemently denied this.

A few days after he had restocked the shop and had it refitted, he suffered several fits of paralysis, in which he could not move a muscle and could barely breathe. Believing that Alice's dire threat had come to pass, the medium decided to come clean, and began telling his clients that he was not psychic after all and that his paraphernalia was worthless. Almost immediately his health was restored and he shut up his shop and moved away from the area.

Unfortunately, I know of many mediums who are fraudulent and have no scruples whatsoever. They think nothing of fleecing highly vulnerable people, who have lost loved ones, and are desperate to make contact with them. I no longer believe in any practising stage medium, and I do not recommend them.

At the time of writing, a young child named Madeleine McCann is missing. She was probably abducted from her bedroom whilst on holiday with her parents in Portugal. The whole world was touched by this abduction, and the parents are obviously hoping (as we all are) that Madeleine is still alive. On the radio I called on mediums everywhere to try their utmost to locate this missing child, and not one of them succeeded. Madeleine is still missing. The same is true of Genette Tate, a thirteen-year-old girl who went missing whilst doing her paper round in Devon, in 1978. The disappearance was reported over the length and breadth of the country, and people suggested using mediums, but again without success. Genette is still missing.

A few people got in touch with me to say that they had foreseen the death of Princess Diana, but only years *after* the event. One of these people argued with me until he was blue in the face about his alleged powers of seeing into the future, yet he had to cancel his flight to the United States, later that week, because he had not foreseen something as global and massive as the September 11 terrorist attacks! The next time there is a major act of terrorism, or a devastating natural disaster, just wait and watch; the self-proclaimed mediums and psychics will crawl out of the woodwork to claim that they had foreseen everything.

A few years back, the Ministry of Defence spent eighteen thousand pounds on an experiment to see if psychics or mediums could identify the contents of a sealed envelope; not a single one of them was able to do so. In May 2008, new legislation was brought into being to combat the enormous number of fake mediums ripping off gullible consumers. The EU Unfair Commercial Practices Directive laid down a code of practice, which forbids all mediums and psychics from coercing or misleading vulnerable consumers.

So beware, if you have lost a loved one, or would like to know about your future as regards to health, wealth and romance, use your own intuition, which is often a reliable guide, because there are many disgraceful fakes out there. By the same token, if you set aside a quiet place in your home, and regularly allot a portion of your time to contacting a loved one who has passed on, they may get in touch if they so desire and think it will help you. Sometimes they will come to you in dreams, or will manifest their presence in little incidents that may at first be mistaken for coincidences. The important thing is to open your mind. If there was a strong bond of love between you and the person who has passed on, please remember these words: It's never over.

TWO LOVELY BLACK EYES

Upton railway station has undergone many changes since it
was first opened in 1896. It once had a quaint booking office
on the bridge that spans the two tracks, as well as waiting
rooms, but the office and the rooms were demolished in the
early 1970s, when the northern terminus of this line was
changed from New Brighton to Birkenhead North. Eight
years after the change, the terminus was changed yet again,
to Bidston.

One autumnal evening in 2006, twenty-two-year-old
Manor Green woman, Clare Whitlock, was waiting in the
shelter at Upton Station, waiting to catch the train down to
Shotton to visit an aunt, when there was a sudden
downpour. The rain hammered on the roof of the shelter
and lashed the Plexiglas windows; a real winter rain, Clare
thought. There was no one else around to share the
cheerless scene, but amidst all the din caused by the rain
pelting the shelter, Clare thought she heard a sigh close to
her left ear. She spun round – to find no one there. No one
in the shelter, no one on the platform. Yet the sigh had been
so close she had almost felt the breath on her neck.

Having checked again, to make sure that she was alone,
she took her Apple iPod out of her pocket and put on the
earphone inserts. She played a few tunes on the MP3 player
to keep her company on that lonely station, yet the memory
of that sigh was all too real and would not leave her.

She was tapping her foot in time to one of the songs,
when she happened to glance through the rain-slicked
window of the shelter. She could just make out the dark
outline of a figure standing in the shelter on the other side
of the tracks. She immediately tried to reason with herself

that the sigh must have come from this person. Sound does seem to travel further at night – but surely only in the dead of night – came a nagging voice from within. Indeed, how could a mere sigh, the softest and quietest of all human sounds – travel across the railway tracks, especially during a noisy downpour?

Clare was still anxiously pondering this question in her mind, when she popped her head out of the shelter to look along the tracks, fervently hoping to see the lights of her train. But the track was still empty, and the skies were darkening with ever more heavy rain-laden clouds.

The song 'Sometimes You Can't Make It On Your Own', by U2, began to play on the iPod, and not being in a mood to listen to that melancholic tune, Clare was about to skip to the next track, when she suddenly noticed that the figure on the opposite platform had now gone. Then, in her peripheral vision field, she noticed someone tall in dark clothes standing to her left – inside the shelter. She turned and saw a woman, well over six feet in height, dressed all in black. Her face was an unnatural grey colour, and her abnormally large bulging eyes filled Clare with terror. It wasn't just that they were coal-black; they were lifeless, unseeing like a doll's.

In that split second, Clare had a flashback of a motorist she had once seen lying dead in the road after a car crash, when she was eleven. She had been unable to avoid looking into his eyes; dead, lifeless eyes, exactly like the eyes of this female stranger.

With the image of those eyes still boring into her brain, she ran out of the shelter and out of the station through the blinding rain and didn't stop running until she was almost home. She was completely soaked through, although she wasn't aware of that until she was safely inside her parent's house. She gave a garbled version of the weird encounter to her father, who tried to reassure her that she had merely seen a Goth; they loved all that white make-up and heavy black eye liner – it was all part of their image, he said. Clare would have none of it. She had never seen anyone with eyes like that – except that poor dead motorist from so long ago.

Clare still shudders when she talks about the creepy incident today. She is convinced that she met a ghost in that shelter, and believes that the long ankle-length skirt which the apparition wore was from the Edwardian or Victorian eras. When I showed her a sketch of a ghostly woman in black seen on nearby Windermere Road, just a stone's throw from the railway station, she held the drawing with a tremor in her hand. The sketch had been made by a student named Jon Moody, who almost collided with the eerie figure one spring morning in 2003, as he went on his morning jog.

At around 6 am, Jon was running around the corner of Windermere Road, ready to turn into Noctorum Avenue, when he startled an almost identical outdated woman in black. She seemed to be staring intently at the house on the corner, but jumped when she saw him. He apologised for almost running into her, but when he noticed her unearthly-looking eyes, he ran off a little faster than he normally would on his morning jog.

At my request, Jon later made a sketch of the strange woman. Clare said the figure Jon had drawn was strikingly similar to the image of the ghost she had seen, from its quaint hat, right down to the long black skirt, and she remarked, "Oh, I wish you hadn't shown me that, I'll have nightmares now." She then handed the sketch back to me, as though in itself it could harm her.

I mentioned the encounters with this ghost on the radio one evening, during a programme about local paranormal encounters, and received many letters and emails from people who had also seen and heard things they couldn't explain at Upton station.

One woman, a pensioner named Mrs Rogers, had once seen someone's exhaled breath condense on the glass of the railway station's shelter and an invisible finger had then drawn a triangle.

On another occasion at the shelter, a mother and her young daughter heard someone singing, even though the station was apparently deserted. What song did this incorporeal crooner sing? Well, from the fragmented recollections of the witnesses, it seems it was 'Two Lovely Black Eyes' – a Victorian song popularised by Charles Coburn, a music hall singer and comedian. Just whose ghost was singing that music hall song in the shelter, and why, is anyone's guess.

PHANTOM FOOTSTEPS

This is another railway mystery, which took place in April 2003, when two seven-year-olds, Mike and Tobias, got off the train at Rock Ferry at around 11pm, after an evening out with two girls in Liverpool. The teenagers distinctly heard someone shout the name "Seddon" to them, as they walked along the platform. They turned round and saw only an elderly man walking with his head bowed against the light drizzle. It soon became apparent that this man wasn't the source of the cries.

Then there came the sound of heavy footsteps coming down the platform – with no accompanying body. The footsteps passed by the old man and gave the two youths the jitters. They quickly left the station and made their way to their homes on Bebington Road, with the ghostly footsteps following them all the way. On several occasions during the ghostly pursuit, Mike and Tobias clearly heard the same voice they had heard on the platform shouting "Seddon".

The young men split up upon reaching the roundabout; Tobias went left and Mike went right, with the invisible pursuer choosing to follow Tobias. He quickened his pace, and the footsteps quickened to keep pace. The panting teenager could even hear the footsteps coming alarmingly close as he frantically inserted his key into the front door. He managed to negotiate the lock and slammed the door shut behind him. Without taking off his jacket, he hurried into the kitchen, where he told his elder sister Rose about the spooky incident.

Brother and sister then heard a single hard rap on the front door. Both crept into the dark hall, and watched the letterbox flap lift up twice and drop after a few seconds, as if someone was trying to spy on them. Then silence ...

On the following evening, Mike and Tobias were so afraid of encountering the phantom stalker again, that they got off at Green Lane station on the way back from Liverpool and walked an alternative meandering route to their respective homes.

I have since learned that, in late October 2002, a thirteen-year-old girl named Vicky, who had gone out Trick or Treating on her own, was approached by a tall man in black on Clyde Street, about twenty yards from the steps leading to Rock Ferry railway station. The man had sidled up to her and asked, "Can I be your friend?' in a rather upper class accent, but Vicky had recoiled from him and had the sense to call out to a passing woman.

At this, the man retreated a few paces away from her and

then darted around a corner. It was then that a second older woman, who had been walking up nearby Bedford Road whilst all this was going on, threw her hands up to her face and stared in disbelief at that corner. After a few moments, she hurried over to Vicky and the first woman and said she had just seen the man vanish into thin air – one second he was there and the next he was gone.

Both women urged Vicky to go home immediately, as she was the one the ghostly character had approached. She took their advice, but on her way home, she heard footsteps following behind her and a gruff voice muttering something she couldn't understand. As soon as she reached her home on Tennyson Avenue, she screamed and hammered on the door, because the footsteps were now almost upon her and were accompanied by heavy breathing sounds.

When Vicky's father came to the door and saw the state she was in, he assumed she had been followed by a living person, not for one moment suspecting that a ghost was the culprit, but he too heard the muttering sound very close to the front door. He called out for the person to show himself. There was no reply – just the sound of the eerie footsteps walking away. Only then did he realise that something highly unusual was going on and he had to admit, despite a lifetime of scepticism – that the footsteps had almost certainly belonged to a ghost.

Just exactly whose ghost stalks people as they make their way home from Rock Ferry station, and the identity of the mysterious Seddon, remain two baffling mysteries.

I Dare You!

For various reasons, all the names and many other details have been changed in the following story, but the story is true nonetheless.

In 2003, thirteen-year-old Ben became besotted with a very attractive fourteen-year-old called Amanda. they both lived in Wirral and went to the same school. Amanda already had a boyfriend of her own age whose name was Adam, and was only too well aware that Ben and her many other admirers burned with jealousy whenever she kissed him in public – which she frequently made a point of doing. Not only was she an extrovert, she was also an expert tease and something of a sadist, who took great delight in tormenting those who longed for her.

Ben spent the whole of that summer thinking of nothing but Amanda, and his mother was forever telling him to set his sights a little higher than the local 'brassy-faced' troublemaker. Ben bumped into her at a bus stop one day and could barely contain himself when she deigned to talk to him. They chatted about the usual teenage stuff – Play Stations and iPods and songs she had downloaded on her pink laptop – and she made out she was only with 'Adam the Goth' because he was going to be the next Slash Rose with his fabulous guitar skills.

"I play the guitar ... only acoustic though," mumbled Ben meekly. Amanda hadn't even heard him, but she did hear him when he offered to loan her two Play Station games and quickly took him up on his offer. Like an eager puppy, he ran round to her house with them at the earliest opportunity and was crestfallen when boyfriend Adam answered the door. He took them off him and closed the door in his face without even saying thank you.

A fortnight later, without so much as a nod of recognition from Amanda in the interim period, Ben spotted her walking down a corridor in school. Taking a deep breath, he walked up to her and trying to sound as casual as he could, asked for his games back. She looked at him as if he was an insect that had just crawled out of the woodwork and said she couldn't find them.

Ben made the mistake of telling his mum about the games and she went on the warpath to Amanda's house and, as they say in Liverpool, 'made a holy show' of her son. Amanda sulkily handed the game discs back, although they were scratched and lacking their jewel boxes. At school the next day, she told everyone about Ben's mum, and not only called her a "skank", but also said Ben had no idea how to act around girls.

One of the boys at the school, Gary, had recently had a bereavement; his grandfather had passed away, and word quickly got round that the dead man had been put in an open coffin in the front room of Gary's house. This was true. Gary's grandfather had been laid out in the coffin for the weekend before the funeral, which was due to take place on the Monday. Such a laying-out of a corpse is an old Irish custom, and Gary's grandfather had been an Irish Catholic.

As these rumours about the body in the open coffin were doing the rounds, Ben happened to be walking home in front of Amanda after school one late afternoon, when she suddenly trotted up to him and whispered in his ear, "Ben, can I talk to you for a minute?"

"Talk about what?" said Ben, more wary now and sensing a trap, and he kept on walking.

She reached out and held his arm, and that slight physical contact was enough to make his stomach lurch. He stopped and looked at her flawless pouting lips, her cheeks like petals and her long glossy hair and he was hooked.

Amanda was a born flirt and had a way of smiling that virtually every boy in the school found irresistible. She smiled that smile at poor defenceless Ben and led him across the road to a telephone box like a lamb to the slaughter. The other children released a chorus of ooohs and aaahs but Amanda just swore at them and told them to beat it.

Inside the telephone box, she looked Ben in the eye, and in her most seductive voice whispered, "I know you want me, Ben."

Ben went red from his scalp to his toes and he felt strange fluttering sensations all over his body. He thought he was going to melt.

"Will you please do something for me that Adam wouldn't do?" she cooed, and she put her palm on the side of his face and gazed deep into his eyes.

"Like what?" mumbled Ben. It all felt like a dream.

"I want you to take a picture of Gary's granddad with your mobile."

"Huh?" Ben was confused. Then it suddenly dawned on him what she meant. She was asking him to take a picture with the camera on his mobile phone of Gary's grandfather, as he lay dead in his coffin. Although he was consumed with love for Amanda, he felt he could not do something as sick and morbid as that.

"Nah, I'm sorry, I really couldn't. Gary's my mate."

She kissed his forehead and whispered, "Oh, come on, you could do it for me, couldn't you? Dare you!"

There was a loud bang on the window. One of the schoolkids had thrown a stone at them. Amanda pushed open the door and screamed a string of profanities at the stone thrower, and perhaps it was being reminded of her ugly side at such close quarters that finally brought Ben to his senses. He was out of his depth and he knew it. He needed to leave, but as he tried to get out of the box, Amanda grabbed the lapels of his school uniform and wheedled, "Aw, you're not leaving me, are you, Benny?"

Ben nodded sternly and undid her fingers from his lapel. As he walked away she bawled after him. "You little creep! Stupid little mummy's boy! You'll probably send your mummy to my house again! Ooh! I'm scared!"

By the time Ben got home that afternoon he was so choked up he could barely talk. He certainly couldn't eat his tea, and at 7 o'clock he left the house by the back door and aimlessly wandered the autumn streets. He came upon Amanda and Adam kissing outside a chippie, and even though he knew he was making things worse for himself, he couldn't help but follow them, even though it cut him to the quick to watch. It was a Friday night, and he had heard from his friends that Amanda's parents would be out until the early hours, and that he would be alone with her. The thought of him touching her and being able to kiss those exquisite lips, filled him with a painful mix of emotions. Having watched them enter the house, he then saw her draw the blinds in the kitchen and their silhouettes meet as they kissed.

Having tortured himself for over an hour, Ben ran off and kept running, until he was out of breath and bent double with a stitch in his side. When he looked up, he realised that he was near the house of his schoolmate Gary. He saw that the curtains in every window of the house were drawn, but the front door was ajar and there was candlelight in the front parlour, where the body was rumoured to lie in the open coffin. Ben felt for the mobile phone in his pocket and took it out. Perhaps he could take a picture of the … No! He pushed the despicable thought from his mind, and set off for home. His sister saw that he was upset and took him to her room, where the whole sorry story came pouring out, including the bit about Amanda's sick request.

Ben's sister was worried that the situation could quickly escalate out of control. Ben was too young and too innocent to be dealing with the likes of Amanda. She thought long and hard about what she should do and eventually, because she knew that Ben could not resolve it by himself, she told their mother, and that was the last straw.

On the following day, Ben's mum went to see Amanda's parents and warned them to keep her well away from her son. Ben cringed with shame and felt physically ill when he discovered what his mother had done. He knew that he couldn't go into school on Monday – or possibly ever again – because Amanda would tell everyone that his mother had been round to her home. They would all take her side because she was the queen bee – popular because everyone was afraid of her – and he felt that he was nothing.

On the Sunday evening, Ben could think of nothing else but what he would have to face the next day. After tossing and turning for what seemed like half the night, he eventually fell asleep in a deeply depressed mood. He woke up at four in the morning and thought he had left his computer on, because the room was bathed in a blue light. He looked over to his desk, expecting to see his monitor aglow, but instead, he saw a weird bearded face, floating in mid-air, and surrounded by rays of light as blue and clear as a summer sky. He froze and felt ripples of fear run over his body. The mouth of the ghostly head opened and closed, and a soft comforting voice inside his own head said, "Go to sleep, Ben. You're a good lad. Go to sleep."

The head then seemed to shrink and fade at the same

time and the blue glow petered out with it. Ben got out of bed, turned on the light, and looked at the point in mid-air where the apparition had hovered. All the fear had gone, and all he felt now was amazement. He sat up in bed for a while, almost convincing himself that a dream had somehow overlapped his waking life, but he knew that he really had seen that glowing head. He went over the comforting words it had uttered, and when he turned out the light the black mood had left him. He went back to sleep and slipped into the world of dreams and contentment.

Then Monday morning arrived, as real and disagreeable as sugarless porridge. He had forgotten all about the phantom bearded face from the middle of the night, and showered in a despondent mood. Even though he dragged his heels, he reached the school gates before the bell and prepared himself for the shame and humiliation which he was sure would quickly follow. However, he was pleasantly surprised to find that Adam was not present at morning assembly, nor did he turn up that afternoon either. Amanda seemed different as well. She seemed in a daze at playtime; no flirting or showing off, and even though she noticed Ben, she said nothing about his mother's visit.

A few days later, an intriguing story began to circulate the school. Adam had wormed his way into Gary's house and taken a picture of the boy's grandfather on his mobile phone as he lay in his coffin, and had meant to send the photo to a few of his friends, on the orders of Amanda, who had egged him on to carry out the sick dare. But the picture could not be sent for some reason. He tried and tried again, but without success. On the night he took the picture, he had browsed through the photographs he had taken of Amanda and then looked at the picture of Gary's grandfather. The dead man's eyes were wide open on image, and he had a big smile on his face. Adam dropped the phone as if it had bitten him. After he had recovered somewhat, he tried to delete the picture, but it could not be erased. All throughout that night, even when the phone was switched off, it would vibrate, and slowly move along the floor towards Adam. Little gasps and unintelligible whispers were heard to come from it. Adam found the whole thing so creepy, he crept downstairs and threw the mobile into the wheelie bin in the back garden. Feeling relieved to be rid of the thing, he jumped back into bed only to find that it was on his pillow, along with bits of foul-smelling garbage from the bin.

Now he really was scared and he pulled on his clothes and walked through a downpour to Amanda's house to tell her what had happened. It was the middle of the night and her father answered the door. He listened to Adam's weird story and concluded that the lad was on drugs and told him to go home.

On that Monday morning, Adam was found sitting cross-legged in the corner of his room under a duvet. His eyes were rolled back into his head, and he was shaking a leaf. His parents could get no sense out of him and he was taken to hospital.

When all this reached Ben's ears through the school grapevine, he thought the version he had heard was all the result of Chinese whispers, but he later discovered from various people, including his parents, that it was true in every detail. Adam went into a coma for almost a week, and during that time his heart stopped twice and had to be restarted with a defibrillator. When he finally regained consciousness, he said that whilst in the coma, he had had a single long nightmare, that seemed to go on for days, and in which he was stuck in a coffin, continually gasping for air. He kept trying to get up but he couldn't, because of the very limited movement of the coffin's interior. Then he had awakened in the hospital. Adam admitted that he had succumbed to pressure from Amanda to take the photograph of Gary's late grandfather on the accursed mobile. It had all been her idea and he had only agreed because he was infatuated with her. The awful events that had followed had made him see her for what she was – a spiteful manipulator, who used her good looks to twist people round her little finger. He never had anything to do with her again, and to this day, Adam won't use a mobile phone.

Gary was more than a little upset by all this and he and Ben supported each other for the rest of their schooldays. When he saw the framed photograph of Gary's grandfather that his mother had put in a frame over the fireplace in the front parlour, he recognised him at once. It was the very same bearded face that had appeared to him in his bedroom, at four in the morning offering words of comfort ...